D1452575

Tales from Wide Ruins

Tales from

Wide Ruins

Jean and Bill Cousins, Traders

Edited by Mary Tate Engels

— Texas Tech University Press —

This book was set in ITC New Baskerville and Lydian and
printed on acid-free paper that meets the guidelines for
permanence and durability of the Committee on Production
Guidelines for Book Longevity of the Council on Library
Resources. ⊗

Printed in the United States of America
Book and jacket design by Lisa Camp

Library of Congress Cataloging-in-Publication Data

Cousins, Jean, 1916-1993.
    Tales from Wide Ruins: Jean and Bill Cousins, traders / edited by
Mary Tate Engels.
        p.   cm.
    Includes bibiliographical references (p.   ) and index.
    ISBN 0-89672-368-2 (alk. paper)
    1. Cousins, Jean, 1916-1993.   2. Cousins, Bill, 1909-   .
3. Indian traders—Arizona—Wide Ruins—Biography.   4. Wide Ruins
(Ariz.)—Biography. I. Cousins, Bill, 1909-   . II. Engels, Mary Tate.
III. Title.
F819.W415C68   1996
979.1' 37—dc20   96-2260
[B]   CIP
96 97 98 99 00 01 02 03 04 05 / 9 8 7 6 5 4 3 2 1

Texas Tech University Press
P. O. Box 41037
Lubbock, Texas 79409-1037 USA
1-800-832-4042

Dedication

Dedicated to the memory of Jean Cousins, who had an insatiable curiosity about life, was always optimistic, was a darn good trader, and had a vision for this book before anyone else.

COUSINS GENEOLOGY

Includes only those generations and family members named in *Tales from Wide Ruins*

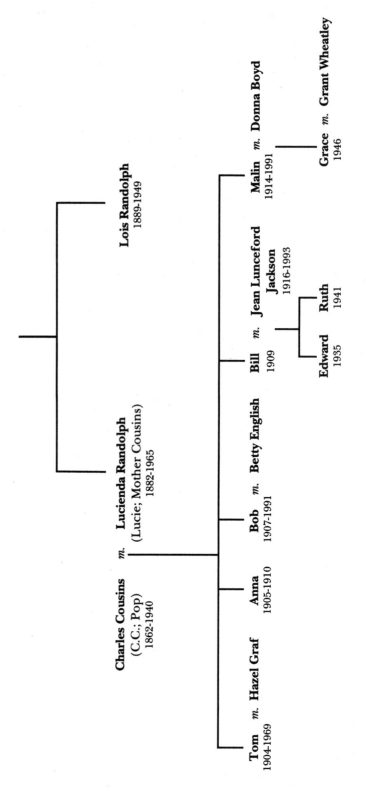

Acknowledgments

Thanks are due to the following for their continued support and assistance on this book. The Cousins family, especially Ruth and Bill, worked tirelessly to finish this manuscript and who provided the photographs from the Cousins's family collection. Brent Engels's editing and observations were valuable. Shane Engels loaned me his computer when mine died midway through this project. Roger Engels, whose support was constant, as always, and drove me on the frequent trips between Gallup and Tucson. Jerry Freund promoted this project from the very beginning and loaned me his research library of Southwestern books; assisted in numerous ways, including leading a trek to the location of the Wide Ruins Post to walk among the spirits and become convinced this project had to go forth; took the photos of the Wide Ruins rugs; and underwrote the color signatures. Sally Freund painted a beautiful watercolor impression of the old Wide Ruins Post, bringing color to our only black-and-white image. Steve Torregossa loaned us the use of his photography studio. Bill Lee kept us all in touch through e-mail. Travis Mayhall designed the map of the areas where Jean and Bill Cousins lived. Mark Sublett of Medicine Man Antique American Indian Art, Tucson, and Pat Messier of Morning Star Traders, Tucson, generously provided assistance, information, and antique Wide Ruins rugs for photography.

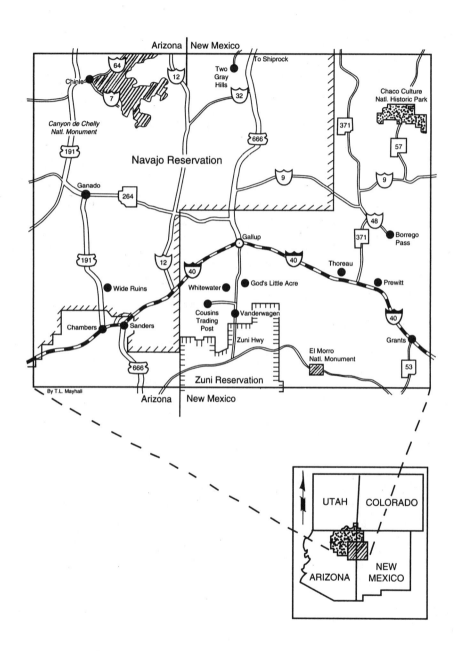

Contents

Contents

The Indian Trader

We hear, if you please, that ther're some who contend
That the trader is not the Navajo's friend!
That his goods are too cheap and his prices too high,
That he cheats on the things that the Navajos buy.
They say that he carries an inferior grade
of the Navajo dyes, that they surely will fade
when used to dye yarn of wool or mohair
for the rugs they are making,
for the Non-Joshie [Gallup] Fair.

But what can he do, any more than advise
the weavers to make their own native dyes?
Nor should he be blamed, when they refuse,
because they have no dye-stuff to use.
He is criticized, too, for the blanket's design,
whether it's coarse, or whether it's fine,
it's never just right. But this I'd make plain—
those patterns are formed in a Navajo's brain.

Oh! The trader is cussed for this and for that.
If the Navajos are thin, or if they're too fat,
if they are lazy, or blind, or halt,
somehow it is always the trader's fault.

Ah, well! It is true, as someone else wrote
that where there's a critic, there must be a goat.

The Indian Trader

But, if it's the facts you're wishing to know
just go to the home of the poor Navajo.

This Navajo family has many sad ills.
They have tooth ache, and head ache, fever and chills.
They have coughs and colds, and eye-trouble too.
And of deaths from TB, there have been quite a few.
For aid and for comfort, in seasons of stress,
where the Navajo goes, I think you can guess.
He begs from the trader, his private supply,
of castor oil, iodine, or drops for the eye.
Then, when death occurs in a Navajo clan,
the person who pays, is this same trader man.
A spade, a coffin and burial robes, too,
of beads and of bracelets, he donates a few.
Then the Navajos, a four-day fast to save,
often ask him to kindly dig the grave.
For weddings and feasts, for chants and for sings,
he donates their food and various things.
He carries them here, he carries them there,
with never a thought of charging them fare.
He pleads for water development,
with everyone sent from the government.
For water, as each and everyone knows,
is the greatest need of the Navajos.

Now, the trader is stern, and the trader is grim.
No, you'd better not try fooling with him.
For he lives in the land where the rattlesnakes grow,
and he fights for the rights of the Navajo.

When the Navajo family awakens at dawn,
and finds that their flour is nearly gone,
that the corn is low in the old corn bin,
that their sheep are much too thin,

the head of the clan pulls his shoes on his toes,
and hastily dons his best Sunday clothes;
on his pony he leaps, to the trading post he speeds
and there, asks the trader for all that he needs.
For tobacco, for seed corn and high-waisted jeans,
for a fat chunk of pork, to cook with his beans,
for a can full of chili to season his hash,
for clothing, for credit, and oft-times for cash.
For certainly, surely, the Navajo knows,
that the trader will furnish all his supplies,
from shoes for the baby, to the Navajo dyes.
And take for his payment, just any old thing,
a ring or a bracelet or a belt or a string
of Navajo beads—white, red or blue,
to hold in pawn for a lifetime or two.
Or perhaps the rug is the item of barter,
made by the Navajo's wife, or his dar'ter.
If the trader is lucky, he'll sell it someday,
and thus, eventually, get square on his pay.

Oh, the trader is poor, his taxes are high,
but still he keeps on—he hardly knows why.
His pleasures are few, his critics are many.
Of civilized comforts, he has scarcely any.
He and his family must live all alone,
not even the land in his yard is his own.
To church or to lodge, many miles he must go.
For neighbors, he has only the Navajo.
But Navajo needs are troublesome as any.
They have wool, rugs, and pelts, but seldom a penny
to bring to the trader to exchange for foods,
so, a market he finds, for these Navajo goods.

O'er mountain, o'er valley, in desert or town,
he's solving their problems; he can't turn them down.

The Indian Trader

Whatever his station, his wealth or his fame,
what matters to him is, "playing the game."
And tho he is blamed for this and for that,
you'll find him there, behind the bull pen,
When the trader grows old, and his hair turns gray,
they'll carry him off, in a box someday.
But to whatever land he may chance to go,
he'll still speak a good word for the Navajo.
And yet, if you please, there are some who contend,
that the trader is not the Navajo s friend.

Anonymous

Foreword

The greatest favor that Cozy McSparron ever did for us (and he did many) was to suggest that we hire Bill Cousins. My husband, Bill Lippincott, and I had become friends with Cozy and his wife, Inja, when we were in the National Park Service stationed at Canyon de Chelly. Cozy had the trading post at the entrance to the canyon, and it was he who talked us into buying such a post when we resigned from the Park Service. Under his guidance we bought Wide Ruins.

As we were complete greenhorns at the trading business, Cozy thought that we would temporarily need the help of a completely reliable and knowledgable assistant. He highly recommended Bill Cousins, who had once worked for him. So Bill and his wife, Jean, came to Wide Ruins when we first moved there, and they proved to be absolutely indispensable. The word "temporary" was dropped, and the Cousinses stayed as long as we did. Their name seemed somewhat confusing to the Navajo customers, who finally settled it in their minds that they were relatives of Bill Lippincott, Bill's cousins.

Both Jean and Bill had grown up on the reservation, and both spoke Navajo—a distinct advantage, as at that time few Navajos spoke English. Jean was a sprightly redhead who nothing ever seemed to faze. Bill was a tall, lanky man, easygoing unless someone violated his strict code of ethics. If a Navajo was the transgressor, Bill usually saw humor in the situation, and so did Jean. Crip Chee, a devilish old troublemaker, tried their patience many times. But Crip had a sense of humor, too, and his practical jokes were so ridiculous that he set the whole store to laughing.

Bill was tall, six foot three, with legs so long that he would stand behind the high store counter and negligently rest one foot on top while he surveyed the Indian customers in the bull pen. That was his usual stance.

He was always quietly cheerful, except on gray, damp, miserable days, when he would periodically mutter to himself, "Dern the weather." When customers demanded his attention, he would unwind his slim body and slowly but gracefully fill their needs while Jean bustled around him. We set up a dartboard at one end of the store to while away idle moments, and Bill always won, because he could almost reach the target from the throwing point.

Bill Cousins thoroughly understood the rug improvement project that we instituted, and he and Jean were the ones who put it into daily practice. Once, driving north on that rutted dirt road toward Klagetoh, Bill looked out to the wide expanses to the west and remarked in surprise, "Those horizontal distances and those pastel colors look just like a Wide Ruins rug."

Sallie Lippincott Wagner

Prologue

In the Bull Pen

"I didn't know I was passing into living history," Jean Cousins said with a laugh. She had read an article about the decline of the old-time trading posts and how they would soon become extinct. Those few posts still functioning in the Southwest were described as "living history."

The memoirs of Jean and Bill Cousins give us original accounts of life during the heyday of trading post development in the Southwest and evoke the sense of actually being there. Alternating dual viewpoints, they reveal the business and personal sides of the people who lived and worked at the remote posts, their methods and motivations, as well as their compassion for people and appreciation of the Navajo culture and art.

In the 1930s and 1940s, well-known posts such as Hubbell's, Cameron's, and Carson's thrived with business between traders and Native Americans. Other old-time posts, such as Cousins Brothers, Thunderbird, Borrego, and Wide Ruins, provided the livelihood and historical arena for Jean and Bill Cousins. They spent more than twelve years at the Wide Ruins Post, known originally as Kin Teel, rearing their family, trading with the Navajo people, and helping to develop the Wide Ruins-style rugs.

Like the complex and fascinating Navajo rugs, the traders' lives are interwoven with engaging historical figures in the Southwest. The Wide Ruins rugs feature designs within bands of color created entirely from all-natural dyes, using none of the commercial aniline dyes popular with other style rugs. The Cousins memoirs capture the variety, texture, and tone of trading life before and after World War II. Their lives are patterned with people who sought the freedom and challenge of Western living, and together they form an important component of the whole story of Southwestern history.

Jean Cousins grew up in the 1920s at Chin Lee, Arizona, playing with trader Camillo Garcia's children and artist R. C. Gorman's family. She often visited "Uncle John" Wetherill, who, with his brother Richard, explored great Anasazi ruins like Mesa Verde and later built a successful trading business at Kayenta. Dr. C. G. Salsbury, who established the Sage Memorial Hospital and Nursing School at Ganado and did so much to improve the health status of the Navajo people, was Jean's personal physician and family friend.

Jean married Bill Cousins, who grew up near Gallup in a family of traders. Bill's father, Charles, participated in the Geronimo campaigns and was involved in a life-threatening incident at Chin Lee Trading Post in 1905. In 1927-28, Bill's Aunt Lois Randolph became the first female state school superintendent in New Mexico, and Bill's career provided a working relationship with many old-time traders like A. J. Newcomb, Cozy McSparron, Bill and Sallie Lippincott, and John Kirk. Bill Cousins's stories are well-honed from a lifetime of trading and "shooting the bull," often as a participant in the trading post's central social area, called the bull pen. Sparked with wit and wisdom, a little yarn and a lot of fun, Bill's tales are lively and entertaining. Yet, he reveals the complexities and struggles of the trading business, especially during World War II.

Jean tells of family life and the growth of a young woman from the innocence of childhood to a successful entrepreneurship in the trading business. Jointly, the Cousinses reveal fascinating lives and insights not previously told, each with a differing point of view. More than anything, their narratives are real, firsthand accounts, and the images they evoke are viable links to the past.

As their stories unfold, let Jean and Bill transport you back to a slower time. Dare to touch the past through them. Join the trail of curious visitors—Europeans, salesmen, artists, and tourists—to the old-time posts. Listen, and you can hear the sounds of children, both Navajo and Anglo, laughing as they play around the post. In the distance, a Navajo sings in his native language as he rides his horse home at dusk. The smell of fresh-cut watermelons in summer and the distinctive fragrance of cedar fires in winter still linger. Step inside the trading post to the inviting aroma of a pot of freshly brewed Arbuckle's Coffee, always ready to welcome the next traveler.

A young Navajo woman offers a rug, small but beautifully woven in the pastel colors of natural dyes. She needs money for supplies for her family. You make the exchange and cling to the rug as she chooses what she needs from the shelves that encircle three sides of the bull pen. You run your fingers over the rug, touching the finely woven strands, knowing you hold a part of her life.

Move closer to where the potbelly stove roars red-hot when the high winds howl outside. Navajos gather with traders and anyone who happens by, teasing each other, laughing at well-worn jokes, regaling whomever cares to listen with tales of adventure and legend.

Read this book as if we were gathered in the bull pen of an old-time trading post, sipping hot coffee, listening to tales from Wide Ruins and beyond, first in Jean's voice, then in Bill's. Step into the traders' living history.

Mary Tate Engels
December 1995

Roots

We can only imagine what really inspired Cordelia Lunceford to leave her family and security in Oklahoma and head west searching for a better life for herself and her child. How difficult it must have been for a single mother to rear a child in 1925. What a remarkable, strong woman Cordelia must have been to strike out on her own and even fight a child custody battle with her own father. If only we had her journal, how much more of her inner strength and motivations would be revealed. But all we have is the view of her through the loving eyes of her only daughter, Jean.

Cordelia's perseverance to obtain an education instilled that same quest for a lifetime of learning in her daughter. You can see the child observing and remembering details of her first trip west and the early Intertribal Ceremonial in Gallup, New Mexico, an event that still occurs yearly and is one of the largest gatherings of Native Americans for cultural exchange and art exhibition. Jean recalls details of the historic El Navajo Hotel in Gallup, and the famous Harvey Girls, who staffed the restaurants owned by Fred Harvey across the West.

El Navajo, which once fed up to twelve hundred train passengers per day, fell to wrecking crews in 1957 to make way for widening U.S. 66.

A strong inner strength can also be seen in Bill Cousins's mother, Lucie. She overcame great hardships to make a home for her family in the remote and rugged Southwest in 1903. The Perry incident at Chin Lee is documented in McNitt's *The Indian Traders* in greater detail. Here we have the Cousins family version that recounts only what is known by them.

Bill's father, Charles Cousins, soldier of fortune and adventurer, established his fame in the Southwest as a strong man and a fair trader. He was well-liked and trusted by his Navajo neighbors and customers. And he learned their language and cared for them. Determined to make a good life for his family in the Southwest, Charles refused to leave, even when most would have pulled up stakes and moved on to an easier life.

The Western spirit of independence and tenacity is evident in both of these families and gives us a little background to the same spirit apparent in their children, Jean and Bill Cousins.

The Way to Indian Country

I never knew my father. He deserted us when I was a little over a year old. Mother and I lived with Grandpa and her two younger sisters, Alice and Ruby, while she attended a teacher's college in Ada, Oklahoma.

My grandfather, James M. Lunceford, came from Illinois in 1893 to make the homesteading run in Oklahoma's Cherokee Strip. He first settled in Edmond and later moved his family to Sasakwa, a small town north of Ada, where I was born on April 28, 1916.

My mother, Cordelia, the eldest of his five children, was born in 1895. Her mother died the year she graduated from the eighth grade, and Grandpa expected her to look after the four younger children and take care of the home. His word was law and gospel, not because he was cruel or unsympathetic to their needs, but because that was thought to be the proper way to bring up a family.

As long as I could remember, Mother's driving ambition was to have an education. Getting that education was a difficult accomplishment for her, but she persisted. She was always studying or riding on horseback to teach in some little country school. In those days, county schools were dismissed so the children could help at home on the farm for certain seasons. During these times, Mother pursued her education in Ada, staying with a family who let her have room and board in exchange for housework.

Jean (seated child); her mother Cordelia (seated); and two of Cordelia's younger sisters, Ruby (standing behind) and Alice, taken about 1920.

Ada was about twenty miles away, and the Rock Island Railway went through Sasakwa into Ada. On weekends, I took the short train, called the "Katy," to visit Mother. Grandpa would put me on the train with a tag around my neck containing my name and destination. What fun I had on those trips. Sunday evenings my mother reversed the destination, and I was homeward bound. The "News Butcher" sold newspapers and snacks and, to me, was the most intriguing person on the train. Once in a while I had a nickel to buy one of his paper cups of fruit.

Somehow, over the next few years, Mother managed to get enough education to qualify for a teaching certificate. Eventually she earned enough teaching credits to get better jobs at larger schools, and I was able to be with her most of the time. However, her studying never stopped.

About 1923, she took the Civil Service exam for teaching with what is presently the Bureau of Indian Affairs. Upon acceptance, she was sent to Keams Canyon, Arizona, on the Hopi reservation, where she taught adult Navajo students to speak and write English. It was quite a challenge since some of her students were as old as she.

During the time Mother was in Arizona, I stayed with Grandpa and Aunt Alice, his youngest daughter, while Aunt Ruby was in college at Ada. Ruby finished college in August of 1924 and received her teaching certificate. Before she could begin her teaching career, though, she drowned while swimming with a group of young people in Little River. Shortly afterward, Uncle Mark's only son died of spinal meningitis, so it was a very sad summer for us all.

After those tragedies, Grandpa seemed determined that nothing else would happen to his children, and he became a very strict disciplinarian with Alice. She was in her early teens and wasn't about to be so restricted. They had one long battle, until finally she ran away and got married to escape her father's rigid dominance.

Mother was a strong person with a pioneering spirit and was determined to get away and make a better life for herself and for me. In 1925, the Civil Service sent her to teach in Chin Lee (now Chinle), Arizona, near Canyon de Chelly (pronounced "de Shay") on the northern part of the Navajo reservation. This time, she took me with her. We rode the Atchison, Topeka, and Santa Fe Rail Line to Hutchison, Kansas, where I remember seeing the glistening white mounds of the salt mines. Then we moved into New Mexico. I spent most of this long trip being sick as a dog from the constant motion of the train.

After several days of traveling, we arrived at two in the morning at a little settlement in New Mexico called Acomita. The stationmaster greeted the train with his cheery little lantern and helped us into the depot, which was a converted boxcar and quite comfortable. We slept there until Mother's friends came for us the next morning.

The New Mexico air must have agreed with me, because the next day I was fine. We climbed the mesa to the top of "sky city," Acoma Pueblo. There was no road, just a narrow zigzag trail hewn out of solid rock, not even big enough for a burro. The Acoma Indians lived there in two- and three-story houses with ladders leading to the various levels, and they tended little farms in the valley. They got their water from large holes scooped out of the rocks to catch rain or snowfall. Everything that nature did not provide on the mesa had to be carried on the people's backs.

I was impressed with the old Spanish mission, which they told me was built about the time the Pilgrims landed at Plymouth Rock. All the materials for its construction were hauled up the same narrow trail that we followed by Indians who were made slaves by the Spaniards. I remembered Willa Cather's book *Death Comes to the Archbishop* and wondered where the priest was pitched over the edge in the rebellion of 1680.

The view from the top of the mesa was magnificent. I marveled at the vast stretches of land in the valleys below that would become my home in Indian country. But even that wouldn't happen easily, not before a challenge.

In a couple of days, Mother and I made our way to Gallup, where other friends met us and were to take us to her new government job at Chin Lee. It happened to be the third week of August, 1925, and the town was gearing up for the fourth annual Intertribal Ceremonial. This event evolved from a yearly gala the Navajos called Ni-ho-hi, meaning "chicken pull." At one time, they buried a chicken up to its neck and the game was to see who could ride by on horseback and pull it out of the ground. The SPCA stopped the practice.

That week we arrived in Gallup, Indians traveled from far and wide to attend the Intertribal Ceremonial, eager to compete in games and dances. The entire celebration went on for several days, and we could hear their dances going late into the night.

As a child growing up in Oklahoma, I had seen a few Indians, but never like this. Hundreds crowded the streets, and everyone was dressed in his or her finest. Many different tribes were represented, wearing costumes and styles I had never seen before as they marched and danced all the way down Main Street. It was certainly a spectacular sight for this little nine-year-old, red-haired girl.

I had never seen a travois; didn't even know what it was. The Plains Indians brought leather slings stretched between two poles, pulling them or attaching them behind their horses to carry their goods and chattels. Some families drove covered wagons in the parade; others rode on horseback. Oh, they were grand!

In the afternoon after the downtown parade, they held races and a rodeo. There were foot races between the Zunis and the Hopi; both were great racers. Sometimes those poor boys would just drop in the road from the heat and exhaustion. There were tugs of war between the women as well as between the men. The women competed in wagon races, and the men had chicken pulls.

Initially the Indians brought simple arts and crafts to sell or to enter in contests. There were previews of exhibits, and the art show was judged and prizes awarded the evening before the activity started. The performers received a small cash reward and were housed and fed in tents at the edge of town.

Mother and I stayed at the El Navajo Hotel, which was owned and operated by the Fred Harvey Company. The interior was elegantly furnished in a beautiful Southwest style. The Harvey Girls provided gourmet dining on a twenty-four hour-schedule, wearing spiffy black uniforms with white aprons and caps. During Ceremonial time, the girls wore brightly colored skirts and the traditional Navajo fashion of velvet blouse, gathered skirt, and turquoise jewelry.

El Navajo Hotel was a meeting place for the government employees on their infrequent trips to Gallup, and it was here that Mother and I were able to rest after our long train ride from Oklahoma. There was a welcoming committee of seasoned employees to greet the two new teachers, my mother and another woman who also came from Oklahoma, Miss Lottie Glenn. Miss Glenn never got over her love of Oklahoma but spent the next forty years or so in Arizona and the New Mexico Civil Service. She became a good friend who took care of me several times over the years when Mother was ill.

We spent a few days in Gallup, then were met by a kindly gentleman named Dick Dunaway, who had been sent to welcome us and to take us to our new home. The trip to the Navajo reservation was via one of the worst roads we had ever seen. Dick was our caretaker, escort, and advisor. Most of all, to me, he was a big Irish tease. I think perhaps he was chosen for this task because he had a big 1923 Dodge touring car.

After leaving Gallup, we turned off onto a dirt road that would take us the one hundred miles to Chin Lee. This road went over the mountain through a beautiful pine forest to Fort Defiance. From there we went across a flat formation of sandstone rock, much like Sky City, where no sign of a road existed. This stretch was called The Devil's Washboard. It was very bumpy and guaranteed to provoke more motion sickness for me. Finally, at the edge of the sheer stone walls of Canyon de Chelly, Dick stopped and showed us the canyon and cliff dwellings of the famous White House Ruins.

It seemed to me that each step in this wild, arid country was almost to the limit. And now we had come to the ends of the earth. This would be my new home.

Born to Trade

My introduction into the trading life came naturally. My father worked as a trader since 1896 and homesteaded in New Mexico territory. He helped my brothers and me establish Cousins Brothers Trading Post, presently Cousins General Merchandise, located south of Gallup, New Mexico, near both the Navajo and Zuni reservations. The Navajos gave my father several names: Ad-a-kai, meaning "gambler"; Dine Di-bitsai, meaning "talker"; and Bi Lah Klikizhe, meaning "painted hands," from his many tattoos. My mother was known as "Ad-a-kai's wife." Mother, a beautiful and smart woman, raised four sons in this untamed country and suffered the tragic, accidental death of a little daughter.

Pop, as we called our father, lived an exciting and adventuresome life. Born in May of 1862 in Calcutta, India, of Scottish missionary parents, he became a soldier of fortune and joined the British merchant marines. Charles Cousins jumped ship in New York in 1881, became an American citizen, and joined the navy as a sailmaker. In 1885, he switched to the U.S. Army, where he was assigned to the 6th Cavalry to help bring peace and order in the West during the Geronimo campaign.

Pop was an enigma. He always dressed neatly and wore a string tie, but his body bore numerous tattoos, probably relics from his days as a sailor. The tattoos came down over his hands, and we kids, as well as the Navajos, were intrigued by that.

While in the army, Pop served until 1896. He did not often speak of his experiences, but they were stamped indelibly on his mind. When we managed to get him to tell us about those days, we four boys listened with great interest and excitement. He recalled the small village of Tinaja, a few miles northeast of Ramah, New Mexico, where the soldiers discovered people butchered and their bodies hung in trees. The troops found a Chinese man still alive who had owned a small restaurant. Geronimo's warriors promised that if he would feed them, they would not hurt him. Unfortunately, after the Chinaman had fed them, he was taken captive and tied down on a hot stove and left to burn. When the troops came upon him, the poor man begged to be shot. The captain ordered a firing squad for the fellow.

At another place, the army found two men who had been stripped of their clothes and staked out on a red ant hill. They, too, begged for a firing squad. This wish was also granted.

Pop and his troops chased the Apaches south to the border of Mexico. Many times, the soldiers were not allowed to make a campfire for fear of being detected, and the evening meal consisted of hard tack, cold salt pork, and water. They followed the Apaches around the mountains in southern Arizona, bordering Mexico for many days. At one time, the troops were ordered to split and circle around to trap the renegades. But Geronimo was slick. He slipped over the border into Mexico, and from there, he sent out his raiding parties. Finally, Geronimo surrendered to General Miles and was imprisoned.

Not all of Pop's army assignments were as gruesome as the Geronimo campaigns. Once the soldiers were ordered to the pueblo of Zuni to stop the hanging of a person believed by the Indians to be a witch. Only about six soldiers were dispatched, along with a small cannon. Upon reaching the outskirts of the village, the soldiers set up their cannon and gave a test shot. Then, a couple of soldiers were sent into the village to request that the "witch" person be freed, or the village would be destroyed by the cannon. After viewing the results of the test shot, the Zunis were quick to comply with the request, and the fellow was despatched to Fort Wingate to live in a safer climate.

Pop served at Fort Wingate with Lieutenant John J. Pershing, who later became well known as General "Black Jack" Pershing in World War I. A relative of one of Pop's fellow troops was Malin Craig, who later became chief of staff of the United States Army. My youngest brother, Malin Craig Cousins, was named after him.

A young Navajo boy who spent a lot of time at the fort was Henry Chee Dodge, known later as Chee Dodge. He was a bright and able student who eventually became a good businessman and respected leader of his people. Chee was the last "chief" of the Navajos. His daughter, Dr. Annie Wauneka, was also a leader and served on the tribal council.

Pop was mustered out of the army at Fort Wingate in 1896. He saw lots of opportunities in the young town of Gallup, and he liked this part of the world, so he decided to stay. He started a saddle shop, which soon changed to the general merchandise and Indian trading business.

Indian trading in those days was far different from the businesses of today. It was often an exchange or bartering system, and very little cash exchanged hands. The Navajos traded wool, mohair, lambs, rugs, and nuts to the trader in exchange for flour, sugar, baking powder, salt, coffee, or whatever staples or supplies they needed. They bought lots of dried fruit, some canned goods, and almost always some candy for their children. The traders then sold the Navajo commodities to the wholesale houses. These were generally located in Gallup and, to a lesser extent, in Winslow, Flagstaff, and Holbrook, Arizona.

Merchandise for the trading post usually arrived by mule team. Later it arrived by rail. The trains improved and speeded up all systems, including the mail. In those early days of trading, many of the foods were packed in bulk and later weighed out at the post, according to the amount of money or trade the customer had. Sugar came in hundred-pound bags; coffee was in bean form and had to be ground; dried fruit arrived in twenty- to thirty-pound boxes. We had no paper bags yet, so each customer supplied his own method of getting the sugar and other supplies home. Many times he would surrender his shirt to tie the sugar in. Most trading posts were equipped with large coffee mills, and each person ground his own. Then came preground and prepackaged Arbuckle Brothers Coffee.

For us, Arbuckle's Coffee gave a three-way advantage: the convenience of ground coffee, packaged in one-pound bags; a coupon on the side of the bag, making the purchase easier and assuring repeat business; and sturdy wooden furniture from the container. One hundred coffee bags were packed in wooden crates for shipping, and those crates made fine shelves for dishes, books, and whatnots.

Pop and two army buddies, Fred and Bill Van Maul, decided to open a trading post at Nutria, a small Zuni settlement about twenty-five miles from the main Zuni village. Another partner was Charlie Beeson. Soon the partnership broke up when Fred married and moved to a post at Blackrock, near Zuni. Bill Van Maul married and moved to a post at Pinedale, a few miles north of Gallup. And Pop moved to Box S Charlie's Ranch, south of Gallup, presently known as Pinehaven.

Pop's friend Charlie Beeson was from Oklahoma, and on one trip back home, he invited Pop to go along. There he met a lovely young lady named Lucienda Randolph. After he returned west, they carried on a lengthy courtship by correspondence. Finally, in 1903, Lucie came to Gallup to become the bride of Charles Cousins. They were married May 29, 1903, in the home of a friend, B. H. Zahn, by the Reverend George Leo Patterson. Later that year, Pop sold the post to Charles McKittrick, and he and Mother went to Manuelito to work for S. E. Aldrich and Chee Dodge. Here their first son, Tom, was born, April 28, 1904.

In the spring of 1905 Charles Weidemeyre asked if Pop would work for him at the post he had recently bought from Sam Day at Chin Lee (now Chinle), Arizona, located at the mouth of Canyon de Chelly. A post office had been established there in January 1903, with Charles Day as postmaster. In late spring of 1905, Pop left Mother, who was pregnant with her second child, and young Tom in Gallup while he rode horseback to Chin Lee to start his new job and acquire living quarters for his family. A few weeks later, after waiting for better weather, arrangements were made for them to follow. The stage was operated by Mr. Coddington, who owned a livery stable in Gallup.

When they got as far as Fort Defiance, the trader there, Mr. Holloway, told them the road north was still snowbound. So, Mr. Coddington returned his stage to Gallup, leaving Mother and baby Tom with Mr. Holloway and his wife. Another week passed before Mr. Holloway learned that enough snow had melted so that they could continue their journey to Chin Lee. A Navajo man and his team and wagon were hired to take them to Ganado, still about forty-five miles from Chin Lee.

They were off to an early start and, after a lengthy, strenuous day of traveling, arrived after dark at Juan Lorenzo Hubbell's

Trading Post at Ganado. Mr. Hubbell met them and explained that the melting snows and spring rains had made crossing the Ganado wash impossible. He invited my tired mother into his home, and his family made her feel welcome. The Hubbells were well known for their gracious hospitality, so they took care of Mother and the baby. Another week passed before Mr. Hubbell thought it safe to cross the wash. There were no bridges, and the quicksand was quite treacherous. More than one had met disaster there. One of the men who worked for Mr. Hubbell hitched up a team and wagon, and they were off once again for Chin Lee.

It had been such a long time since Mother had left Gallup with the baby that Pop became concerned for their safety. One day, he started riding horseback toward Ganado. That same day, Mother happened to be on the last leg of her long and arduous journey to Chin Lee. About midway, the driver sat up and strained to look in the distance. He said, "I think I see a rider on horseback. Must be the new trader from Chin Lee."

Mother laughed, relieved at last. "If that's the new trader, then it must be my husband."

They settled in at Chin Lee, living right there at the post. Old-time trading posts were usually built with the living quarters attached to the store, and a wareroom for storage separated the two areas. This served the dual purpose of being close to the business and a deterrent to break-ins.

In August of 1905, their only daughter, Anna, was born. Life in Chin Lee was not dull. Adventure and excitement seemed to follow Pop, even into trading. Although he never gave an official interview about it, he and Mother were once involved in a dangerous hostage situation.

During the years of trading with the Navajos, Pop became quite fluent in speaking their language. He was often called on to interpret or to settle disputes. Ruben Perry, the Indian

Charles and Lucie Cousins with children Tom and Anna in 1906, visiting at field matron's house, site of Perry skirmish at Chin Lee. Miss Speer, one of the field matrons, is far left. Far right is Father Leopold.

agent at Fort Defiance, had been sent to Chin Lee to investigate the report of a rape. The Navajo man accused of the crime had been ordered to surrender, which, of course, he refused to do. So, Mr. Perry decided to make the arrest personally and take the man back to Fort Defiance. This action was taking place at the field matron's headquarters, about a mile and a half from the Chin Lee post where Pop and Mother lived.

Pop first learned of Mr. Perry's dilemma when a Navajo man came thundering up to the post on horseback and asked Pop to come to the meeting, as the people were angry and some were threatening to kill the agent! When Pop arrived, Mr. Perry had been dragged from his buckboard and some in the crowd were starting to beat him. In spite of the confusion and noise, Pop was able to determine from a much-frightened Mr. Perry what was happening.

The angry ones were friends of the accused and were demanding his release, and immunity for him and for themselves. Pop told Mr. Perry that he had been a soldier and would help put up a fight, but it would be a losing battle with just the two of them against this crowd. Mr. Perry could see the logic of this and decided to let federal soldiers handle the situation. He agreed to the demands and managed to leave in one piece. Perry filed his report, never mentioning Pop's intervention that saved his life.

All was superficially quiet for two or three days after that, but Pop knew the Navajo people were agitated. Two posts in the area were broken into and robbed on the same night. Sam Day's place at Cienega Amarilla (St. Michaels) and the Cousins place at Chin Lee were the victims. The glass in the pawn case had been shattered, and a hatful of the pawn was scooped out. The thief left no clues, but a few days later, Pop noticed that one of the Navajo men who was lounging around the post wore one of the bracelets that had been taken.

Pop confronted the man: "Where did you get that bracelet?"

"Won it gambling," came the surly answer.

But Pop kept on: "I believe that's one of the bracelets that was stolen from me. You have to return it."

"No!" the man said, and began spitting on the bullpen floor.

Several other Navajo men came into the post, all wearing pieces of the stolen jewelry. Pop was furious and asked them to return the things they took. But they refused. Pop figured it was time for a showdown. He walked from behind the counter and locked and bolted the front door. Then he went back and placed a revolver on the counter in front for all to see and said, "No one's leaving here until the stolen jewelry has been returned."

All morning, as more Navajo men came to the post, Pop would let them in and lock the door behind them. At noon, Mother came to call Pop to lunch, and that was the first time she knew of the serious trouble brewing in the trading post.

Pop told her what was going on: "Go back to the house, lock all doors, and stay away from the windows." She hurried away to protect her baby. I'm sure she was thoroughly scared.

Dark came early, since this happened in the fall, so Pop lit a kerosene lamp around midafternoon. By now, the small quarters, with no ventilation and a room full of men, was becoming pretty rank. Shadows danced on the walls. And tension grew. Suddenly there came a knock at the post door. Cautiously, Pop opened the door, expecting more angry Navajos. Instead, there stood a young cavalryman and a Navajo scout from Fort Wingate. Troops had been summoned earlier for the trouble between Perry and the Indians, but they turned back when that incident was resolved so quickly. However, when the soldiers reached St. Michaels, they learned about the two post burglaries and headed back to Chin Lee to see if everything was all right.

Well, Pop was certainly glad to see those six U.S. Army troops. The soldiers took two of the ringleaders into custody and made sure that most of the jewelry was returned to the showcase.

Later, Pop learned that a group of Navajos on the outside were waiting for nightfall and planned to shoot burning arrows into the building. Pop claimed that he had been prepared to shoot his family and himself rather than let harm come to them at the hands of the Indians.

During the next few years, Pop moved his family to Oklahoma, where their second son, Bob, was born in 1907, and back to Gallup when farming didn't prove profitable. He worked at Mariano Lake, Fort Defiance, Floating Rock, and

Lucie and Charles Cousins with (left to right) Tom, Bob, and Bill at old Vanderwagen, about 1911.

finally homesteaded south of Gallup about half a mile off State Road 32, at a place called Whitewater. The family refers to this place as the Old Homeplace, where Pop established C. C. Cousins General Merchandise. I came into the family December 30, 1909.

The Old Homeplace was the site of many escapades, adventures, close calls, and generally ornery pranks perpetrated by the Cousins boys.

Chin Lee, Whitewater

Chin Lee, in 1925, was a small, remote settlement. Yet many of the residents became known in historic circles. As a child, growing up and playing in and around Canyon de Chelly, Jean touched the family lives of the Garcias, the Gormans, "Uncle John" Wetherill, Dr. C. G. Salsbury, and several veteran traders. In 1923, Pauline and Camillo Garcia formed a tripartnership with Leon "Cozy" McSparron and Hartley Seymore, all traders in the Chin Lee Valley. They kept Garcia Trading Post and Thunderbird Post open at Chin Lee and closed the third post, a mammoth, two-story structure built in 1900 by Lorenzo Hubbell. In this building erected by Hubbell, a young Jean attended school at Chin Lee and, years later, started housekeeping after her marriage. The building was eventually left to ruin, and Lorenzo Hubbell moved on to Ganado and opened the Hubbell Post, which became a successful and famous post that continues to operate today.

The Cousins were busy experiencing the tragedies and triumphs of a growing, rambunctious family. The four brothers learned strong values of helping each other and working together, traits that would last a lifetime. Even as a teenager, Bill was aware of his family's financial situation and developed a strong desire to do something to help. Bill learned the paternal role of trader to the Indians from his father, and this is evident in these childhood tales as well as later in his own dealings with the Navajo.

Willa Chee, "Little Red Ant"

I was very impressed with this new place that we would call home. Mother and I had a bedroom in a building called The Employees Club. There were four bedrooms upstairs plus the bathroom. We had an upstairs room, and Miss Glenn had the only downstairs bedroom. There was also a large parlor or lobby and an even larger dining room, living quarters for a cook, and large kitchen.

All government employees were welcome to take their meals at the club. Many of the employees were single and took advantage of this arrangement because they lived in small rooms with no kitchens that were scattered throughout the campus.

It didn't take me long to make friends with the cook. She was an Indian woman from Acoma and married to a Navajo, who was the school's maintenance man. Both were very good to this little redhead, freckled-faced girl.

I played with the Navajo children as well as the Garcia children and others whose parents worked for the government. Traders Pauline and Camillo Garcia had a daughter my age. I loved Margaret and her two younger sisters, but often fought with her brother, especially on the walk to school every day. We played around Canyon de Chelly and explored the foot trail built by the Park Service from the canyon's rim to the floor near the White House cliff dwelling. It didn't take long for the Navajo children to give me a fitting name, as was their custom. I was called Willa Chee, meaning "little red ant."

I started school the fall of 1925 in the same building where I would later start keeping house, built by Lorenzo Hubbell. My first teacher was a young man from St. Johns, Arizona, but he didn't last out the term. The Anglos did not have a good school year. We were not allowed to attend government-run Indian schools. The following year, Mother was taking no chances of me losing another year of education and made arrangements for me to return to Oklahoma and go to a girl's school run by Benedictine sisters. I learned a lot there but was almost physically ill from homesickness. Although Grandpa didn't live far from the school, I was only allowed to visit him on some weekends or holidays.

At the end of the school term, I gratefully went to Grandpa's for a week's visit. But at the end of the week, he was so happy to have me there, he failed to send me back to Arizona as he was supposed to do. Mother was beside herself. She begged, then angrily demanded that he send me back to her. But he refused. Finally she wrote to a judge she knew in Oklahoma and requested that her father be arrested if he didn't put me on a train for Gallup by a certain time. It was a drastic measure, but it worked. I was on the train, but oh, so lonesome for Grandpa.

For such a remote place as Chin Lee, we had our share of activity and visitors. One interesting arrival was a woman professor from Oxford, England, Dr. Blackwell, who struck up a friendship with Mom. I was such a *smart* kid, telling this Dr. Blackwell how we celebrated the 4th of July, then asking if the English observed it. Mom came undone and sent me to bed in a hurry. I was thoroughly embarrassed.

Dr. Blackwell planned to visit Canyon de Chelly, the White House Ruins, and what we called the Monuments, at the upper end of the canyon. She wanted to ride horseback, probably around thirty-six miles there and back. My mother had done lots of horseback riding, so she volunteered to go along. Dr. Blackwell insisted that Mom ride as the English did, on a small saddle. They rented the ponies from a Navajo man, Nelson Gorman, father of artist and teacher Carl C. Gorman and grandfather of artist R. C. Gorman. Nelson later claimed that the women rode so hard that the dye from the saddle blankets stayed on those ponies for more than a year! Well, they didn't get back until quite late, and my poor mother could hardly walk or sit or do anything but moan.

There weren't many eligible bachelors in Chin Lee, nor much social life. Teachers and matrons were expected to teach the children some of the social graces, so once in a while, they would hold a dance in the school auditorium. The music was furnished by a wind-up phonograph and perhaps some employee who could play a piano. Dances were mostly the Virginia reel and waltzes. The Charleston was popular at that time but hadn't reached Chin Lee. The Indian children were very timid and had to be pushed along to participate in these activities. These affairs were always well attended by employees, missionaries, traders, and anyone else near enough to get there.

Dick Dunaway, the man who drove us to Chin Lee, was a middle-aged bachelor employed in the government reclamation department. It wasn't too long before he and my mother started "keeping company." This wonderful man who kept showing us the cultural points of interest would eventually become my mother's husband in June 1928. This created quite a stir, for some of the traders had eligible women in their families who were interested in him. Now all they could say was, "That widow woman just needed someone to take care of her and the kid."

I was in school in Oklahoma when the marriage took place in the McKinley County Courthouse in Gallup. Some of their friends decided a short camping trip would make a nice honeymoon and all would go along. Lucy Jobin and another teacher, Lottie Glenn, were full of mischief and the instigators of the camping trip idea. They took along lots of mosquito netting and fashioned a bridal veil for Mother. The bride carried a bouquet of sagebrush, and they staged a mock wedding. It was lots of fun for all to remember.

What a great stepfather Dick turned out to be. He was the only father I ever knew, and I loved him dearly. His real name was Nobel Dunaway; Dick was only a nickname. And "noble" he was. He was good to me and Mother's younger sister, Alice, who came to live with us.

Dad, as I called him, was the windmill mender and made monthly trips through the northern and western parts of the Navajo reservation to repair windmills used to pump water for cattle. At first he made these trips with a team of horses and a wagon, his dog, and one or two Navajo men as helpers. It sometimes took almost a month to travel his route, especially if extra work had be to done on any of the mills. About 1930 the government issued trucks for the workers, and he was able to make his route much quicker.

Like all kids, I soon learned to have my way most of the time. When Mother said "No," I managed to get whatever I wanted from Dad. The poor dear must have been overwhelmed by suddenly having a wife, a preteen kid, and a late-teen sister-in-law. Dad always called Aunt Alice his "Tom Thumb sister," as she was only four feet eleven.

There was a little sibling rivalry between us, but certainly no prejudice from my parents. They tried to treat us equally and fairly. Dad built us a rock house with a kitchen at the back but no modern facilities. Our bathroom was an outside privy, in the style of the day. Many years later a bathroom was added and we, at last, had water in the house.

My childhood at Chin Lee was quite a happy one. During the summers I was invited to spend time with several traders. The Frazier family lived at what we called the "valley store." He was a sportsman, and she was a homemaker from Missouri. They had two sons and a beautiful daughter, all much older than I. Mrs. Frazier was a great cook and seamstress, and she had the first swamper food cooler I had ever seen. It was a wooden frame covered with burlap and had a drip system on top.

On occasion, Mrs. Frazier had to take care of the trading post while her husband made a business trip to Gallup. Since the store opened into the living quarters, it wasn't necessary to stay in the post all day. This made it possible for Mrs. Frazier to pursue her household interests and keep an eye on the store at the same time.

Another trader family I visited was Sybil and Howard Wilson at Chil-Chin-Bitoh, meaning "bitterweed water." I liked the Wilsons' place best, probably because they had a small daughter for me to play with, which was a real treat. Sybil did most of the trading because Howard always seemed to have plenty to do in Gallup, which the Navajos called Non-Joshie, meaning "bridge." Sybil furthered my interest in sewing and cooking. They didn't stay at that post long but moved to a store north of Gallup so their daughter could go to school.

The one place that epitomized charm and hospitality was the home of the John Wetherill family in Kayenta. "Uncle John" and his brothers were the first white men in Mesa Verde Ruins, and later John explored Monument Valley, Rainbow Bridge, Keet Seel Ruins and Betatakin Ruins. The Wetherills had spent some of the most turbulent times in Navajo history in their migrations. Uncle John's brother, Richard, settled at

Chaco Canyon and was eventually murdered there. They had traded a while at Dennehotso and later established their place at Kayenta. Their home was the personification of Western hospitality, and many famous people stayed there. They had frequent paying guests also.

One summer Dad, Mother, and I spent about a week or ten days with the Wetherills while Dad was tending mills in the area. The building was long and narrow with a covered porch and walkway the length of it. No two rooms were opened to each other. One had to visit his neighbor by going outside and entering into the next room. A flat roof covered with dirt made the roof and ceiling.

Their home was beautifully decorated in Western style with heavy wooden furniture. The interior walls had been covered with unbleached muslin and securely fastened. A few pictures adorned the walls along with relics of a by-gone era: old rifles, skins, some silver. Mostly, though, the ceilings and walls were hung with Indian baskets. The huge living room had a great fireplace at one end. I was never in the kitchen, but the dining area was long and narrow and looked large enough for twenty to thirty people to eat. When Uncle John was home, his place was at the head of the table and his wife sat at the other end.

Uncle John was a Quaker. Where I came from, everyone was either Catholic, Methodist, or Baptist, and I knew no one who was a Quaker. He might as well have been from Mars. But he was a gentle and loving man to his family and friends. They had adopted two young Navajo girls, Betty and Fanny. I never knew their other children, as they were away at school or living on their own.

One of our Chin Lee neighbors was Carl Gorman, father of the famous artist R. C. Gorman. At that time, Carl was a struggling young man hauling freight for the reservation trading posts and coal from a mine at Black Mesa, about

Jean, age fourteen, on graduation from the Chin Lee Public School.

twenty miles away. During World War II he became one of the Navajo Code Talkers and afterward made his mark as an artist, lecturer, and teacher.

That was a wonderful time in my life. I wasn't aware of it, but a love of God's beautiful world was making an indelible imprint on me that has never ceased to grow.

During the next two years of my grade school, I attended the Chin Lee Public School once again. My mother quit the Indian Service school and went to work for the county, which meant that she had the difficult task of being my teacher for the seventh and eighth grades. Believe me, that wasn't any picnic. I was expected to be the shining example in class, which was a hard role for me. But in retrospect, I wouldn't trade those years for anything. I was the only girl in the eighth-grade class of four and the first girl to graduate from the Chin Lee Public School in May 1930.

Aunt Alice was sent to Santa Fe for nurses' training at St. Vincent's Sanitarium and Hospital. Just a few months short of finishing her schooling, she ran off with and married a man who turned out to be a high-class bootlegger. My, she had some wild rides about the country.

Much to my dismay, I had to spend the entire year after my graduation in bed. Dr. Clarence G. Salsbury was afraid that I was going to have TB, for during the last school year I had endured one constant bad cold and had no energy. After six weeks in the Sage Memorial Hospital at Ganado, the doctor recommended that I spend most of my time in bed, getting plenty of rest and fresh air. I had bathroom privileges, but that was it.

My folks erected a tent in our front yard for me to sleep in and tried to make it cheerful and comfy. Summer and fall weren't too bad, but winter was filled with hot-water bottles, hot rocks, and irons, and so much extra cover that I could hardly turn over. I'm sure that I was a big pain in the arse, but all things come to an end and by the time summer came again,

I was fat, sassy, and, best of all, up and about. I survived that, but it is a wonder that Mother did.

I want to add a word or two about Dr. C. G. Salsbury. He had served as a Presbyterian missionary for about twenty years in China before coming to the Navajo reservation. He worked tirelessly to improve the small hospital at Ganado Mission, finally getting enough commitments to start construction on a new hospital. People from all over the U.S. helped contribute, including the Mayo brothers, and quite a few Navajos. Almost as soon as the Sage Memorial Hospital was finished, the doctor established a college of nursing, encouraging the education of Indians and anyone else who wanted to go.

Dr. Salsbury was sympathetic to the Indian healing and religious beliefs. Strangely enough, a healing ceremony sometimes works. Quite often he would tell a family, "You'd better bring in your medicine man to say his prayers along with my prayers and maybe together we can pull the patient through."

The next fall, Mother found a Catholic boarding school, Sacred Heart Academy, in Waterflow, New Mexico, for me to start my high school years. How she found a Catholic school in the midst of a Mormon community, I can't imagine. I spent two happy years there, then went to Flagstaff, where I attended high school. When I returned to Chin Lee in 1934, my life would change dramatically.

The Shoot 'Em Up Boys

The next year after moving to the Old Homeplace, we lost little Anna. I was just a baby, but the family told me what happened. She was roasting piñons at a campfire when her clothing caught fire. Pop heard her cries and ran to help her, rolling her over and over in the dirt to put out the flames. Croppy, a Navajo neighbor and friend, rode his horse over twenty miles into Gallup for a doctor, but it was too late for her. Little Anna died several hours later, June 13, 1910. She was four. Croppy's horse died, too, from being ridden so hard. In his grief, Pop neglected his own burns, developed blood poisoning and pneumonia, and almost died.

The fifth and last child of Lucie and Charles Cousins, Malin Craig, joined the family in June 1914.

After two or three years, hard work paid off and the store, C. C. Cousins General Merchandise, was doing well. Pop started felling logs to start a new home. But the forest service decided they needed this land, after all. So, once more, the family was on the move. While trying to find another place, Pop moved the family to the old Vanderwagen place, about ten or fifteen miles further south and near Zuni. We stayed there around two years, when my folks received word that they could have the old place back. We moved back and once more began to improve the land and the trading post. This area later came to be known as the Checkerboard Area.

Charles and Lucie Cousins with (left to right) Bill, Tom, Bob, and infant Malin. Below: Charles and Lucie Cousins and children.

The store was right on the road to Zuni, so times were pretty good as more and more white people were taking up homesteads to try and become dry-land farmers in an unforgiving country. In addition to the store, Pop always ran twenty to eighty head of cattle. He also bought about seven hundred to one thousand head of lambs every fall from the Navajos. As kids, we all had horses and gear, but Mother never rode horses. Pop would always hitch up the team to a two-seated buggy for her.

Pop established a post office in 1920. The main office refused the name of Whitewater as there was another place with that name in the state. My folks submitted a list of names, including Cousins, for the post office. And Cousins is the name they accepted.

A white settler named Manion Jones wrote to the post office department complaining that sometimes he had to walk all the way to the postmaster's home for his mail. He failed to mention that it was only next door and usually during lunch time when Pop closed the store. There was no record of the many times he came to Pop's at eight or nine at night for his mail. Anyway, Pop said, "To hell with it! I don't need a post office to get my mail." Since we lived on the Zuni Road, we got mail delivery three times a week.

The people of the community begged him not to quit, but he had had enough. So Mother agreed to take over the job and in 1924 became postmistress of Cousins, New Mexico.

We kids had lots of fun and usually found our own amusement. We were not always the best-behaved kids, and more that a few times, got into trouble.

When Malin was a baby, it was Bob's job to wheel him around in his buggy. Bob, who was seven, always saw to it that I, who was only five, helped with this babysitting. One time when we were wheeling the baby around, Bob asked me to take over so he could go to the toilet in an old outhouse left by the forest service. Really, he wanted to roll himself a good ol' cedar-bark cigarette and have a smoke. Well, after he fired up his smoke, he carelessly tossed the lighted match in a box of tissue paper orange wrappers that Pop had put down there for toilet paper.

In a minute, he came running out and grabbed an old tomato can and headed for the well down in the valley to get water to put the fire out. So I headed for the store and turned in the fire alarm. By this time, it was too late to save the outhouse. For my trouble, I had to spend the rest of the afternoon in bed. Of course, Bob had to go, too, but I thought it was terribly unfair to me, as all I did was turn in the fire alarm. But maybe it made up for all the times I wasn't caught.

We often made our own toys and whittled toy guns to play our favorite, Sheriff and Robber. I was the thief (as usual), and Tom and Bob were the law. They caught me in my hideout and brought me to trial, where I was found guilty and sentenced to hang. One of them climbed up a pine tree and fastened a lariat to a limb. They made me stand on a box with a rope around my neck and somehow, the box got knocked out from under me. They got scared and ran. It just happened that Pop came out the back door and saw me dangling. He came running with his pocket knife out and ready and cut the rope. When he made sure I was okay, he ran after my brothers. He was furious with them, and we never played "hanging" again.

It seems that I was the one to fall for any kind of tricks my big brothers wanted to pull. One time Bob and I were sitting in the three-holer outhouse wearing little loose-fitting cloth hats. Oh, how we hated them. "I overheard Mother and Pop talking and they said that just as soon as we lost these hats, they would get us new cowboy hats," Bob said. "Let's throw these down the toilet."

Boy, I couldn't get mine off fast enough, and down the hole it went. Well, Bob tore out like a streak and told Mother what

I had done. I was in big trouble with her. She even threatened to get the garden rake and fish the hat out and make me wear it. You never heard such begging as I did that day. But it paid off; I eventually got a new hat.

By the time we boys grew up to be school age, Mother's sister, Lois Randolph, moved out from Oklahoma to stay with us. She fell in love with the Southwest, the climate and beautiful sunsets. She taught us the three R's, and a tough, no-nonsense teacher she was. Pop backed her up, so we kids had to do what she said. Later she started the Opportunity School in Gallup, teaching boys and men who couldn't read or write. She also taught many diverse ethnic groups so they could get their citizenship. She was a fine, smart lady and eventually became school superintendent for McKinley County. Later, she was elected state school superintendent.

Finally, there were enough white children in the community, plus a few Navajo children whose parents wanted them in school, that the county agreed to hire a teacher. Pop furnished a building for the school and a place for the teacher to live until the county could build a one-room schoolhouse for grades one through eight with living quarters attached at Cousins.

We formed a baseball team and played baseball every Sunday, when everyone gathered at the school. Eventually it was decided by the community that they should have a church and Sunday school at the schoolhouse. Union Church and Sunday School accepted all denominations, and different ministers would come from Gallup or Rehoboth and take turns preaching. Then, the Baptists went after us with full force and were successful in getting most of the young folks to join the church. Upon joining, we were taken to Gallup, to one of the coal mines where they had some kind of pond. The water was

Charles Cousins on far right, and Bill Cousins, about twelve, in center, getting sins washed away.

about waist deep and we all waded in and were dunked three times. So, we were baptized in the Baptist Church.

The very first Sunday after that, we were playing baseball as usual when the preacher came to the door of the church and rang the bell. We were surprised and went inside, where we were informed that we were not going to be allowed to play baseball on Sunday. And furthermore, there would be no more Saturday night dancing at various houses. Later, we talked the situation over. The next Sunday we were playing ball again, and when the preacher rang the bell, we didn't pay any attention to it. After about the third time, he came out to the field where we were playing and demanded to know what was going on. We told him that we had decided to quit being Baptists, and we did. There was a lot of flack about it, but we stayed quit.

Pop was an expert shot and taught us all how to shoot, as well as safety in handling guns. We all had our own .22-caliber rifles, so every fall and winter we made sure the family had plenty of fried rabbit. One Sunday afternoon, Mother and Pop took a long walk down to the lower pasture, leaving Bob and me home alone. Bob started messing around with Pop's double-barrel twelve-gauge shotgun and loaded it. Then, we realized that we didn't know how to unload it before it was fired. We'd seen Pop unload plenty of times after it was fired, and that's all we knew. "We'll just have to fire it," Bob decided. "Draw straws." Of course, he made sure that I drew the long one, so I was to be the one to shoot it off. We went out back of the barn and I sat with my back braced against the wall. We found an empty half-gallon Dr. Price's Baking Powder can, and I let drive and demolished that can. Bob then realized that I didn't get hurt, so he would try it. He went back into the house and brought out all the cartridges. We loaded up and were having a ball shooting.

Mother and Pop heard all the shooting and raced home as fast as they could. About that time we finally ran out of ammunition, so Bob sent me to the store for more. I rounded the corner and ran right square into my dad. "Where are you going?" he asked.

"After more cartridges," I answered honestly.

"No, by God, you are not!"

We kids never got spanked, but the scoldings we got were severe, and the shaking of Pop's finger in our faces seemed worse than a whipping.

I traded my friend Clifford Quick a pocket knife for an old .22-caliber rifle that needed a new firing pin. I ordered the part from the Remington Company and waited impatiently for what seemed forever for the thing to arrive. Finally, the big day came when the order came in the mail. I installed it with the help of a friend, Paul Dessieux, and at last the rifle was ready for a tryout.

Down under the hill from our home was the old, half-burned, abandoned outhouse. And, like all good outhouses, it had a quarter moon carved in the door. Bob and I decided that moon would make a dandy target. Bob insisted that, since he was the oldest, he should get the first shot. Ready, aim, fire—Wham! As he took aim for a second shot, the outhouse door burst open and out flew oldest brother Tom, pants at half mast, hollering, "Don't shoot!" It shook us up to think we could have killed our own brother in the outhouse.

At school, the boys decided to have a race for a Barlow pocket knife. A few of us devilish fellows took a sack that was supposed to hold the knife and filled it full of fresh cow manure. Then we buried it. The first one to race fast and reach it would get that knife. The smallest kid in class took off like a shot and ran ahead of everybody. He really wanted that knife. When he reached the part of the sack sticking out of the ground, he yelled, "I've got it!" and started digging as fast as he could. Then he discovered it was just a sack of manure. "Ahh!" he said, furious with us. So we gave in and handed him the Barlow knife he'd really won.

Pop decided to have a well drilled closer to the house, as the well we were using was way down in the valley and you had to use a bucket and rope to get the water. He hired a well-driller from Gallup to bring his rig out and start drilling. They used a large gasoline engine to power the rig. Gasoline came in five-gallon cans that were square, and there were two cans per case. There were lots of empty cans piled up, so our oldest brother, Tom, decided to make a steam engine, using one of those cans for the boiler. We built a fire and he set the can on the coals while Bob and I were getting snow to poke down into the can for the water. Before we got back with the snow, Tom could hear something sizzling in the can, so he looked into it. But he couldn't see anything, so he struck a match to give him a little light. Immediately there was a big boom and Tom took off, running around the chicken yard.

Bob and I tried to catch him to see if he was hurt. When we finally caught up with him, we thought he looked pretty bad. He was all black and his eyebrows and lashes were burned off and blisters were starting to rise on his face. We talked the situation over and decided the best thing to do was for him to go into the house and wash the soot and blood off so we could see just had badly he was hurt.

Mother, figuring something was wrong, wanted to know why he was washing between meals. She took one look at him and saw that he'd been cut as well as singed. Fortunately we had a phone and she called a doctor at Blackrock, near Zuni, who gave her instructions for taking care of him. Tom later became Gallup's fire chief for several years, but he carried the scar to his grave.

When I was a kid, about ten or eleven, I tagged along with Tom and Bob and another neighbor boy. We decided to pull a dirty trick on one of the neighbors, a real nice young man. There was a new schoolteacher at the county school at Cousins who lived in the teacher's quarters there. She was young, good-looking, and very nice. The young man came courting one night, driving his Model T Ford. Model T's didn't have batteries and had to be hand cranked. They had a magneto, and there were a series of magnets on the flywheel. If I remember right, this magneto would put out about 2,200 volts of electricity, but hardly any amps, so to boost up the current to where it would give enough power, it was run through four coils. They were situated in a metal box under the dashboard. The metal box was fastened to what I would call the firewall. The box was about ten inches long by four inches wide and eight inches deep. Contact was made through the bottom of the coils.

We cut out a square of oilcloth that would fit nicely in the bottom of the coil box, took the coils out, and put the oilcloth in the bottom of the box. (Oilcloth was what a lot of people used for tablecloths, especially on kitchen tables.) When this poor fellow came out to start his car, he cranked for about a half hour. The schoolteacher, Miss Cloute, finally suggested they go back in and she would make a cup of coffee. He did this and while he was inside, we took out the oilcloth.

When he came back out, he took one pull on the crank and the engine started right up. He then proceeded calling his car all kinds of names, saying there wasn't anything as contrary as a Model T. Which was about right, except we were worse.

Pop didn't like to drive. Once, he started to learn to drive and drove so fast from Gallup to home that he scared himself. When he saw how fast he'd been moving, which was only about 35 mph on a very rough road, he swore he'd never drive again, and he didn't. 'Course, top speed was about 50 mph on good roads. But he bought a Model T Ford which became my responsibility to drive and keep up the repairs. I was about twelve.

Pop, for all his tough-soldier image, was a compassionate man and couldn't stand to see the children coming to school during the severe winters without warm clothing. So he extended credit to the parents of these children, even though he knew they would never be able to repay. That, along with the loss of many cattle due to heavy snows and the Indian people moving into the hills, combined to make his merchandise business a nonprofitable endeavor.

Pop began looking for another spot to file for homesteading. Since he had only filed on a quarter section the first time,

Original ranch that Charles Cousins built.

Pop Cousins on porch of his ranch house at Cousins, New Mexico.

he was allowed to file on another one hundred and sixty acres within a certain distance of the first place. Eventually, in 1925, he found a beautiful place, a little north of Zuni, with huge oak trees and an apparently bountiful supply of water. This was to be the final quest for a family home and became known as "the Ranch."

Pop dug a well about ten miles west of the Old Homeplace at Cousins, New Mexico. They reached water at about twenty feet, so he homesteaded there and, as time and circumstances permitted over the years, built a beautiful ranch-style home. This later became the location of the Cousins Brothers General Merchandise store and post, which has been in the Cousins family for seventy years.

One of our neighbors was a Navajo family that we called Pinto, because the man rode a paint pony. By Navajo standards, he was wealthy, with five thousand head of sheep and lambs, two to three hundred head of cattle, and about a thousand horses. This family became friends and worked with and helped my family for many years.

The trader was often called on to bury members of a Navajo family. Our neighbor George, Pinto's son-in-law, and his horse were killed by lightning when he tied the horse to a metal-wheeled wagon in front of their hogan during a rainstorm. The family asked Pop to bury him, and they had been friends, so of course Pop went up and got the dead man, made a coffin, dug a grave, and buried him. A few years later, the man's widow, Pinto's daughter, also died. Once again, Pop was asked to bury her beside her husband. Pop promised Pinto that he would take care of those graves, and he did. The family rode by regularly on horseback to make sure the graves were undisturbed and still all right. They wouldn't get close, just near enough to observe, then would ride on.

The Indians trusted Pop, and when you have someone trust you like that, it's important to do what they ask. You take care of them. I could go right to those graves today at the ranch, if I could walk that far.

When the Indians didn't have a trader to take care of the bodies of someone who died, they would put the body in the hogan and tear it down all around, then set it on fire. They would burn it all completely. They would shoot the person's horse and just let it lay there and put the saddle under a tree and just leave it there. No Navajo would bother it, because they knew it belonged to a dead man. Only a white man would dare to remove it, and not many of those.

We respected the Navajo and their culture. There were a few saddles lying under trees at Wide Ruins in 1937 and 1938. They were old, nearly disintegrated saddles, but nobody touched them. Navajos were highly superstitious of lightning, coyotes, bears, fearful of death, snakes, and a house where someone had died. They always buried the nicest items with their family members—jewelry, baskets, buckskin, anything the person might need for the journey to the next life. They killed the horse so it could go along and provide a ride into the next life. Some might consider robbing graves of their treasures, but not those who know or respect the Navajo people. Turquoise, when buried in a grave, turns a terrible green, and no one wants it. Silver turns dark and buckskins and baskets disintegrate.

Pop tried dry-land farming, but we struggled because there was no money in it. He harvested lettuce, tomatoes, peas, radishes, squash and other garden produce, but there was no sale for it. We just had to eat it all. We raised barely enough hay for our team of horses and stock. We grew enough oats, corn, beans, and chickens, but we needed flour, sugar, coffee. Those items were hard to come by. By then, Pop was on a

"Wild" Bill Cousins, about fifteen.

small Indian Wars pension, and that was supposed to support the family. But it wasn't enough.

Bob went to work on the railroad and Tom found work in town. Both of them helped out with what money they could spare from their meager wages.

When I finished school, I was about fifteen years old. I wanted to do my part for the family, so I went into town, to Gallup, to get my first taste of working for the other fellow. I applied at the Puritan Bakery, delivering groceries in a Model T Ford delivery truck, but Tom told the manager not to let me have that job because I didn't know how to drive. This wasn't true, because I'd been driving since I was twelve. He also said that I didn't know the town very well, but I knew it well enough. When I didn't get that job, I was really burned up about it.

Tom was working for Nelson Apple of Sinclair Oil Company. Mr. Apple said, "Young man, if you really want a job, you can come in and work for me." Well, I wanted that job, so I went into town and stayed in Tom's bedroom at the Apple house. My job was to help with household chores, like breakfast and dinner dishes, cut kindling, get coal ready for the furnace the next morning, and chop firewood. After that, I would sometimes help at his office. The first of the month came along, and I didn't get a paycheck. I went to Tom and asked, "Did Apple pay you?"

"Oh, yes."

"Funny, he didn't pay me," I said.

"He ain't gonna pay you," Tom explained. "You're just working for your room and board."

I was sure put off. "He never did tell me that. He just told me he'd give me a job."

"Well, that's all you get. The job and your room and board."

"Hell, I had that at the ranch." I went back to the living room and sat down, studying this situation. But it was soon clear to me.

Mr. Apple came in and said, "Young man, in the morning, we're going to do . . . so and so at work."

Without thinking, I said, "No sir, in the morning, I'm going back to the ranch."

Mr. Apple and Tom though that was funny, because there wasn't a car available to travel the thirty miles to the ranch. Besides, it was spring and cool, and the road was muddy as hell. They thought it a big joke that I might try to walk it. I never said another word about it.

Next morning after breakfast, I helped with the dishes. Mrs. Apple said, "Nelson is ready to take you to work."

I answered, "I'm not going to work. I'm going to the ranch."

Pretty soon, Mr. Apple came stomping in and said, "Young man, are you coming to work?"

"No," I said. "I'm going to the ranch."

Well, he got in the truck and took off. And I put on my jacket and started walking. About four o'clock in the afternoon, I came in sight of the old house at Cousins, New Mexico, about twenty miles from Gallup. Our friends, Mr. and Mrs. Charlie Davis, were living there at that time. Mrs. Davis looked out the door and said, "Someone's walking up the road."

Mr. Davis said, "Looks like Bill Cousins." After a little bit, he added, "It is Bill Cousins."

Mrs. Davis got busy and said, "I'm going to fix him something to eat." She gave me a plate of beans, biscuits, and fried eggs. I'd never tasted anything so good in my life. And I'd never been so tired in my life. Mrs. Davis insisted that I spend the night: "You're not going to walk down to the ranch tonight. It's at least ten miles." The next morning, she fixed me a nice breakfast and I took off and walked on home to the ranch. And that was my first miserable experience working for the other fellow.

Thunderbird Post, Chin Lee

This tender love story shows how quickly Jean and Bill Cousins moved into adult responsibility. While their families were supportive, financial assistance was limited. Jean's schoolgirl innocence changed to the dutiful roles of wife and mother in less than a year. Bill's personal obligations to his parents shifted to his own family, and dealing with unemployment became a constant struggle. Jean's undiagnosed case of scarlet fever and the subsequent spreading of the disease reveal the medical risks of their time and place. In her accounts, Jean frequently mentions being thankful for good health, something she did not take for granted after surviving her various illnesses.

Ironically, the Thunderbird Post, where Bill's father, Charles, encountered the Perry incident at Chin Lee in 1905, was the place where Jean and Bill met in 1934. The home that Charles built at the ranch, the Cousins Brothers store, and the road that Bill surveyed are still in use today. Many of the early posts reported a "spy" character, someone who went from post to post claiming that the other one sold an item cheaper, thus serving to advertise the competition. We can see how many of the Native Americans were given names by Anglos who couldn't pronounce their Navajo name or merely chose a descriptive word, like Fussbuttons or Croppy.

Leon H. "Cozy" McSparron was a veteran trader who became famous for his tours of Canyon de Chelly, and Bill liked working for him. Both Cozy and his wife, Inja, worked with the Navajo weavers to develop a better rug by encouraging them to return to the old vegetal dye methods used prior to the introduction of commercial dyes in 1880. Most of the Chinle-style rugs contain a combination of vegetal and commercial dyes to make the colored bands and stripes on a borderless pattern. The McSparrons' ideas later influenced their young friends, Bill and Sallie Lippincott, to develop the Wide Ruins all-vegetal dye rug style.

Interestingly, Jean's view of Cozy and his wife, Inja, was somewhat different from Bill's. And moving on to another job after their marriage just seemed the right thing to do.

Falling in Love

I returned home to Chin Lee from school the last of May 1934, feeling very sophisticated after being more or less on my own in Flagstaff for a year. Chin Lee was abuzz with young men that summer. There was a handsome new clerk at Thunderbird Guest Ranch and Trading Post, plus six or eight surveyors who were working on a topographical map of Canyon de Chelly. One by one, I met the guys, and, since there were only a very few young people, we all got together for picnics, moonlight rides up the canyon, marshmallow roasts, and card games. All of a sudden the guys left me completely alone and stopped calling on me. I was dismayed, not to mention lonesome after all that attention. Much later I found out why.

After work and before dinner, the guys all gathered in the bull pen at the Thunderbird store, where Bill Cousins worked. The bull pen was the area in front of the counters, usually around a pot-bellied stove, where folks liked to socialize. One of the fellows said he was going to ask me for a date. Bill, the new clerk, reached under the counter and pulled out his revolver and laid it on the counter and said, "Leave her alone, dammit. She's mine!"

Very effective! They left me alone.

Several days passed before I heard from Bill, and then it was indirectly. For all his boldness in the bull pen, he became mighty shy to ask me for a date. The cook at the guest ranch called and said that Bill Cousins would like to play tennis with me if I was free. At that time, I didn't even know who Bill was!

In the next few months, I got to know him well, and by July, we were so in love. When we told Mother and Dad, they asked that we wait until September to see if we still felt the same. Well, we waited, but of course, our love was stronger than ever.

Bill had been made receiver of the Thunderbird Guest Ranch and Trading Post and was quite busy, but evenings we would go riding in Bill's truck. It was one of the first Ford roadsters. Bill tried to hard to teach Mother to drive, bless her. But that was a losing battle. She never learned, much to her chagrin, saying, "Every other woman could drive, but I can't." She was too excitable and nervous. She would come to a bridge and turn out and end up in the ditch, explaining she wanted to "let the bridge go by."

My parents were very strict, and I had to be home by 10 PM Sometimes Bill and I played cards at some of our friends' homes at the Chin Lee Boarding School, and there were dances two or three times a month. Other than that there wasn't much to do, so we would go riding through the round-topped hills in the area known as the Chin Lee Mounds. We noticed that Mother and Dad followed us occasionally, so we would drive to the top of one of those hills and park. From there we could see them looking for us in all the nooks and crannies. When they headed back, we would leave and beat them home. They were always so surprised to see us there first and asked where we had been. "Oh, just riding around," was always the answer. They never did know until after we were married that we dodged them on purpose.

Bill and I were married at the mission in St. Michaels, Arizona, on September 10, 1934. Members of both our families were there, and Bill's Aunt Lois and my uncle stood with us, since Dad couldn't attend.

We did not have a honeymoon because Bill's employers, Mr. and Mrs. L. H. "Cozy" McSparron, who were owners of the Thunderbird Lodge, were a little miffed that they were losing their efficient, charming bachelor help. Mrs. McSparron decided that this was a good time for them to visit relatives in Kansas, so Bill had the complete responsibility of the Thunderbird Post and only one day off. Because of that, we promised ourselves a delayed honeymoon.

After our wedding, we went into Gallup and had our photographs taken. We did a little grocery shopping, then went back to Chin Lee. We knew that some of our friends had planned a shivaree for us. They were waiting until our lights went out to create their havoc, so we fooled them. Bill put the gasoline lantern in the clothes closet and slowly shut the door, making it look as though we had turned it off. We didn't have to wait but about five or ten minutes when the dish pans and cow bells began outside. Everybody was surprised when we came to the door fully clothed and with a lighted lantern. They stayed until about eleven, enjoying coffee and cake. When they left, Bill brought out some booze (illegal on the reservation) and we had our own private party until the wee hours.

Our new residence was an old building that had been built in 1900 by Juan Lorenzo Hubbell. It was first used for a hotel, since there were always tourists coming through and needing a place to spend the night. In the 1920s, they used it for the schoolhouse, and that was where I had started to school in the fall of 1925. It seemed strange to be setting up housekeeping there.

The building was quite large, with the lower part used as a trading post and hay barn. The upstairs had sixteen bedrooms and one very large room, measuring forty by forty feet. This must have been the hotel lobby. The next room, formerly the hotel dining room, was twenty by forty and functioned as our living room. The next two rooms were about twenty by twenty each and comprised our kitchen and bedroom.

Believe me, our first home was sparsely furnished. Mother had given me a three-quarter-size bed and a chest of drawers. The place came furnished with a cookstove of sorts, a built-in dish cupboard, and a dry sink. For a couch we had a discarded church pew with no padding. Bill's boss, Cozy McSparron, gave us a large Navajo rug for a wedding present, which we used as a couch cover. It looked fine until someone sat down, for it was quite hard and slippery on that old church bench. Mr. McSparron also loaned us a huge round dining table and four chairs.

This building had been constructed before the days of inside plumbing and central heating, so Bill had to haul all of our water. Obviously we used it sparingly. For a bathroom, there was an outdoor one-holer, which we reached by negotiating a steep set of steps in the yard.

Our large home was located on a small hill, and across the way lived a Navajo family. The head of this family was a very old man who everyone called Squinty. He was most adept at stealing from our wood pile. We had to pay twenty dollars per cord for it, and in 1934, that took quite a chunk from Bill's wages of ninety dollars a month plus room and board.

In September 1934 I received a wedding greeting from my old friend, Mrs. Salsbury, wife of Dr. C. G. Salsbury:

Dear Mrs. Cousins,
    Please accept our very hearty good wishes for your happiness in all days to come.
    After years of happy married life, we desire that all enjoy the bliss that we have known for 25 years. I think that we both agree that the only way to be serenely happy is to always think of the best for the mate. This works both ways. The wife

should always think of her husband's comfort and happiness before her own and the husband also seek to give his wife every thought that will make for her happiness and comfort. After all of these years, we feel that the plan has worked and we are more in love with each other than at any time in the past.

We hope to see you from time to time. Living near us, you will likely pass by Ganado and we hope that you will stop and see us once in a while.

With greetings and all good wishes in which my husband joins me, I am

Most cordially yours,

Cora B. Salsbury (signed)

On Christmas Day that year, I went to bed with something called quinsy, which was a severe throat and tonsil infection. I remained bedfast until the first of February. We found out much later that my quinsy had, in fact, been scarlet fever. When I was able to be up and about, Bill decided to take me out to his folks' place, which we called the ranch, so his mother could help me recuperate. Meantime, Bill had also had this fever, only this time it was diagnosed as wood fever. His head swelled so much that his eyes were almost closed. I think he stayed home from work for only half a day.

We didn't know it, of course, but we were quite contagious. Bill's younger brother, Malin, and his mother came down with the fever. The Cousinses' family doctor diagnosed us all with scarlet fever then. Between the two of us, Bill and I could have wiped out all of Chin Lee.

Struggle to Work

When I was about seventeen years old, in 1927, I got the bright idea to start a trading post. I thought I knew all about the trading business. So, I approached Tom with my idea. He said, "If you make the adobe bricks and build it, I'll furnish the lumber for the roof, windows, and door for the store." Well, it was no easy chore, but we did it. One wall was crooked, but we finally got a roof on it. When it was finished, it was a pretty good building. Tom wanted to go into the sheep business, so I bought about one hundred head of ewes from the Navajos and ran them with the Indians herds. Eventually I gave Tom some money and all of the sheep for his share in the store and I became owner of Cousins Brothers.

The road to the Zuni Highway (Highway 602) wound around for twelve miles and was in terrible condition. I asked the county surveyor to survey a straight road the seven miles to the highway, but he couldn't do it then. He told me the degree off north that the lines ran, and a friend, Walter Florence, and I rigged a compass, tripod, and plumb bob and proceeded to survey that road. We went to the southwest section corner of Pop's land and started east. We hit every section corner except the last one right on the nose and decided to go ask the farmer if he had moved the corner stone. He denied it. Finally, we put a jog off the right of way.

The Indian Service agent at Fort Defiance gave me one hundred dollars to hire Indians at a dollar a day to help chop the timber and clear the right of way. Then, there were all those stumps to clear out. I again went to one of the county commissioners and asked for dynamite, caps, and rolls of fuse. He okayed the order and gave me seven cases of dynamite. So, I started to blow up the stumps. I loaded the Model T with the dynamite, caps, and some tools and stopped about 150 feet from the first juniper stump, which was a real big one. I dug down a few inches and took a stick of explosive and punched a hole in it about the size of a pencil lead, attached two feet of fuse, and lit it. The boom was loud, but the stump stayed right there. I realized that I had to dig deeper and put in more powder. So I did. I tied six sticks together the next time, lit the fuse, and hurried back to the Model T. My God, what an explosion! Pieces of that stump must have gone three hundred feet up into the air. Chunks of wood fell all around me while I was running as fast as my two legs could go.

The noise flushed out a neighbor half a mile away. Jerry Matajcich came rushing down. "My God, man. You're going to blow us all to kingdom come! And look at all the dynamite you wasted." Fortunately, he had been a powder man at the coal mines near Gallup and was an expert with explosives. He took over the job and finished clearing out the stumps. I was only too happy for him to do it.

Then the county sent out a crew and they graded the road, put in some culverts and a couple of small bridges, and we had a much better road.

We didn't call Cousins Brothers a trading post, even though Navajos were our main customers. From the Navajos we bought lambs in fall, wool in late spring, fine rugs, blankets, and jewelry made by their silversmiths. Also, we bought anything else they had to sell, like corn, beans, and piñon nuts. Then we had to find a market for the products. It wasn't easy.

Most of the time we sold to the wholesale houses in Gallup, like Gallup Mercantile and Gross Kelly.

The spy was a Navajo man about eighty years old who had a small farm near our place at the ranch. Pop nicknamed him "the spy" because he went from trading post to trading post and claimed, "They're selling coffee cheaper over there," or, "Beans are cheaper over yonder." Malin traded the spy a bunch of groceries for a six-shooter. Later, Malin was bragging about his good deal. I teased him, "If you make many more deals like that, the spy will own the store."

John Fussbuttons, whose Navajo name was Tse Codi Bi Doni, was always hanging around the store. We called him Fussbuttons because his father had that name for always fussing about everything. Later, John Fussbuttons changed his name to Tom Robertson Smith.

When John was about sixteen, he wanted his hair cut. Most of the Navajo men at that time wore their hair long, but he wanted to be different. So I cut it for him, pretty dang short, and he was tickled with his new look. But his mother, "Old Lady" Fussbuttons, was furious and chewed me out good for that.

Chip, my second cousin, whose parents had died, came from somewhere in California to live with us at the ranch for a few years. Chip knew nothing about the Navajos but was fascinated by them. At Cousins Brothers General Merchandise, the Indians had free use of the well and often came there for water. One day when we were standing near the well, John Fussbuttons came to draw water with a bucket and rope. He looked at Chip and said, "Toh" (pronounced "toe"), which means "water" in Navajo.

Chip didn't understand his meaning and looked concerned and asked, "What's that? What's wrong with your toe?"

We all got a big laugh out of that and teased Chip about toes for a long time afterward.

One day, one of the spy's kids came running into the store and said, "Our father's dying! We moved him out of the house because we don't want it to be chindi [haunted]." Pop went over there and found that they had the old man wrapped in some blankets, lying in some bushes.

He was furious. "You get your father back in the house," he said, "and I'm bringing some medicine." Pop figured that the spy had pneumonia, gave him some medicine, and the old man got well. He lived well into his nineties.

Many women in those days took Lydia E. Pinkham's compound because it was supposed to make you fertile. People claimed that there was "a baby in every bottle." A young Navajo, Joe Mance, a son of the spy, and his wife had been married a few years and didn't have any children. He asked Dad if there was some medicine he could take to help the baby situation. Dad said, "There's something your wife could take. They say this'll help." And he gave them a bottle of Lydia E. Pinkham's. So the couple took the bottle, and away they went with their horses and wagon. Within a few years, they had a whole bunch of kids, so I guess it worked.

One day a young Navajo man came into the store and asked, "Where is your father?" I didn't speak the Navajo language very well at that time but could get along in the store okay. I couldn't hold a conversation with anyone. I went to get Pop, who could speak excellent Navajo. The young man told Pop that there was a certain girl that he wanted to marry and she wanted to marry him. But their parents and the head men of the tribe wouldn't allow this marriage. Pop told the young man to go home and tell both their parents and the head men of the community to come to the store for a meeting. Then he told the young man, "Of course, you and the girl can get married."

The next morning there were about twenty or twenty-five Indians sitting outside the store. Pop went out and asked the young man in Navajo, "Why won't they let you and her get married?"

The man piped up in English (no one knew he could speak English), "Because she is my uncle!"

Pop raised both hands and said, "Of course, you can't get married!" And he walked back inside the store. That ended the meeting as well as the wedding plans.

An excellent Navajo tracker lived just a short distance from us at the ranch. His name was Croppy because of the way his hair was cut. Most Navajos of his age wore their hair long, but his was cropped short.

Aunt Lois owned a section of land nearby and a little two-room cabin. She didn't live there all the time and hadn't been back in about six weeks. This is the same place (God's Little Acre) where, several years later, Jean and I bought forty acres and started a trading post. Anyway, Aunt Lois came to our house all upset, saying that her cabin had been broken into and what the thief didn't take, he destroyed. Dishes, pictures, figurines, everything was smashed on the floor. She wanted that thief caught and punished. So, Bob and I went to Croppy's hogan and asked him to come and track the thief for us.

When we arrived at Aunt Lois's cabin, Croppy walked out about 150 yards and started circling until he found a track. He figured the trail was ten to fifteen days old by then. Bob and I took off with him. Croppy would go at a trot most of the time. After we traveled about a mile and a half, Croppy stopped on top of a small hill. I could see the tracks very plainly going on down the hill. Croppy said, "No, he came back and hid his tracks." I just could not believe it, so I stayed on the trail and followed the tracks down the hill while Bob and Croppy were circling about two to three hundred yards away. Croppy found the real trail, which led in the opposite direction, and they hollered at me. I went over to them, as I had run out of tracks by then. Croppy said, "He stepped on rocks for a long ways, leaving no trail." He pointed out where some of the rocks had been disturbed. We went on about another mile and came to a big arroyo or ditch. Croppy said, "Something is buried in the sand over there."

We dug down in the sand and, sure enough, there was a suitcase. Aunt Lois's suitcase was full of her things. We left it and went on. Just a short distance we came to a hogan. Croppy pointed. "He is in there." I opened the hogan door and walked in. We could tell we were at the right place because Aunt Lois's things were all around the room. We made the thief carry them, as well as the suitcase we had dug up, back to Aunt Lois's cabin. Bob, who was a deputy sheriff, took the culprit to Gallup, where he was locked up in jail. Eventually the thief was found guilty and had to serve some time.

In 1930, the bad economy hit us hard, and I had to take other measures to make ends meet. My first few experiences working for the other guy left such a bad taste in my mouth that I swore I'd never work for another. Sometimes we eat our words, though.

In 1930, the Great Depression was on us, and the bottom dropped out of the market on both lambs and piñons, our main trading sources with the Navajo. Lambs dropped in price from approximately $4.00-$5.00 per head to about $1.50 - $2.00 per head. That broke me. We owed the wholesale house in Gallup about $2,300, so I decided I'd best go out and find work in order to help my family, as well as myself, with the debts we had incurred. I left Cousins Brothers Post in the very capable hands of Pop and Malin.

I went to work at Prewitt Trading Post on Highway 66, about forty miles east of Gallup, and worked ten to sixteen hours a day for seventy-five dollars per month. I sent fifty dollars home and lived on twenty-five dollars a month. At that time, we could buy coffee for ten cents a pound and sell it for fifteen cents, or two pounds for a quarter. We sold a good grade of flour for ninety cents per twenty-five-pound bag. We didn't fool with pennies in pricing, and even laughed at stores in Gallup for charging odd prices like nineteen cents, thirty-nine cents, or ninety-nine cents. Anyway, the Indians didn't understand about counting pennies. If something was ninety-nine cents, they knew that was ninety cents plus nine, and you were adding on to the original price, thus cheating them.

Because our roads were so rough, we had to buy a truck every year. A new Chevrolet pickup cost only a little over seven hundred dollars, so the fifty a month that I sent home more than made the payments on the truck and helped with the costs of supplies we couldn't grow. Our older brother, Bob, who had been working on the Santa Fe Railroad as a fireman, lost his job and went back to the ranch to help run Cousins Brothers. He also used the pickup to haul supplies. He was a very good manager and in a few years got the store out of debt and on its feet.

One Sunday, Mrs. Fussbuttons, John's mother and the one who chewed me out for cutting his hair, came into Cousins Brothers. I'd been gone for a few months working at Prewitt's Trading Post and came back to visit my family at the Ranch and work a little at the store. Mrs. Fussbuttons sure was glad to see me and complained about the way Bob had been treating her. "Your brother is stingy," she said. "I'm sick. I know the government leaves medicine to be given out to the Indians. When I ask for medicine, Bob just gives me just one pill. It isn't enough to do me any good. Would you give me some more pills?"

"Oh yes," I said. "I'll give you some." So I went into the store and got the bottle of compound cathartic pills, and I gave her six. This was something folks took as a physic.

She asked, "How should I take them?"

"Take two now. When you get to the top of that hill, take two more. When you get home, don't take the other two. Wait a day or two and see if you need them because too many will kill ya."

The top of the hill was one quarter-mile away, and she just lived over the hill. I didn't see her for a couple of months after that because I went back to work at Prewitt's. Apparently, she took the two pills when she walked to the top of the hill, and two more when she got home.

Later Bob told me, "You damn near killed that old woman. My God, she was as pale as a ghost for a month after you gave her those pills. You've got to be careful about that."

I said, "Maybe so." I felt real bad about making her sick. Well, "Old Lady" Fussbuttons got word that I was back at Cousins Brothers and came to see me at the store. I saw her walk in and wanted to duck out, but she was tickled to see me and told me that the medicine worked and now she was cured. I was relieved and figured she must have needed those pills.

My duties at Prewitt Trading Post included trading with the Navajos, selling general merchandise, doing maintenance and whatever needed to be done around the post. I only refused to do one job: milk the cow. I had thirty minutes for lunch and generally was off Sundays.

If ever there was a job the traders hated, it was to bury the dead from the Navajo families. While I was at Prewitt, I was called on to bury a little boy who was struck by lightning while herding sheep. A preacher who lived down the road helped me do the work of building a coffin of wood and digging the grave. We put the coffin in the grave and stood back and looked at each other. I finally said, "Aren't you going to say a little prayer, or is it up to me?"

"Oh yes," the preacher said. "I'll pray for his soul." So we had quite a lengthy prayer.

I'd been working there about a year when another trader who ran a store at Cubero came around and visited with Mr. Prewitt for some time. He figured he was pretty smart by taking advantage of the Depression. Seems this trader had two men working for him, and he told them he needed to cut their wages in half or one of them would have to go and he would employ just one. Both men had families, so they took the cut and both stayed on to work at the reduced rates.

I could see that my boss was very interested in this idea, and I made up my mind right then, *no cuts*. Sure enough, after this trader left, Mr. Prewitt approached me: "Hey, Bill, times are sure tough, and I'm thinkin' about cuttin' your wages by one-half. I figure I could easily get a man to work for half of what you're makin'."

My response was quick: "I was under the impression that I'm already working at a cut wage, Mr. Prewitt."

"Think it over, Bill. It might be worthwhile for you to stay employed."

I went back to my room, but I'd already made up my mind. In the morning, I opened the post. When Mr. Prewitt came in, I told him, "I just can't accept a pay cut. I have a family, too. Maybe you should go ahead and get that other man to work for you at half my wage."

He looked a little surprised. "Aw, I'm afraid I wouldn't have him, Bill," he said, shuffling his feet. "I guess we'll just go on, working on the same basis."

"No," I answered, feeling pretty bold by then. "The only way I'll stay on will be with a raise of five dollars per month."

He refused my counter offer, so I left. In about a month, Mr. Prewitt came out to our family ranch to see if I would come back at the same wages for now, and he promised to give me a raise a little later on. Well, by then, I needed the money, so I agreed to go back to work for him. But he never gave me the promised raise.

In 1932, I left Prewitt's Post for good and went to the Two Gray Hills Post, where my next employer was worse than the first. Morris Kirkpatrick was an ornery son of a gun and, without a doubt, Simon Legree personified. His trading business wasn't very good because the Indian people did not like nor trust him.

My first night at the post, I discovered that Two Gray Hills was infested with bedbugs. I sat up on a hard-backed chair all night, keeping the light on, because when the light went off, the bugs came out. The next morning I dragged that mattress outside and set it afire. I then scrubbed the shack and put the legs of the bed in cans of kerosene so those buggers couldn't climb up to where I slept. But they dropped from the ceiling! It took a while for me to get rid of the bugs and make the place livable.

Since I wasn't busy trading, Kirkpatrick had me feeding a flock of chickens, gathering the eggs, cleaning chicken coops, making the mail run, doing general maintenance—anything and everything but what I was hired to do, which was to trade with the Navajos. Each morning I drove Kirkpatrick's Model A pickup truck on the mail run. This meant traveling west about eighteen to twenty miles off Highway 666 to Toh

Adalena (meaning "running water"). There was a U.S. Government day school as well as a trading post and post office run by George Bloomfield. I picked up their mail and took it to Newcomb's Trading Post and Post Office at Newcomb on Highway 666, where the mail truck would carry it on to Gallup. Then I retrieved the current bunch of mail and delivered it to Toh Adalena and drove back to Two Gray Hills with our mail.

One Sunday evening during a pouring rain, a young Navajo woman came just at dusk with two small rugs to trade. Kirkpatrick threw a shoe and ran the woman out after insulting her by offering five dollars for both rugs. When he left, I told her, "I'll give you seven dollars for them."

Poor thing was in tears. "My children haven't eaten all day," she said, "and I've been weaving to get done before night so they could have something to eat. If you would let me have a twenty-five pound sack of flour, pound of lard, pound of coffee, a small can of baking powder, and a can of tomatoes or something sweet, you can have the rugs." She went back into the store and bought groceries with the money I paid for the rugs. Kirkpatrick had already gone to his quarters, so I rang the sales up on the register, then took the rugs and went home.

The next morning, Kirkpatrick was fuming! He demanded that I take back the money and give him the rugs. "No. The rugs are mine," I told him. "I bought and paid for them, and your money is in the register. The rugs are not for sale." Those two rugs went with me several years later when I married and we set up house.

I think even Kirkpatrick's wife must have been fearful of him, for she often said, "Try not to upset Morris. He's ill, you know."

I awoke one morning and decided that enough was enough. So I went to work opening the post and when Kirkpatrick came in, I told him what was on my mind: "I'll give you two weeks of work so you can find other help. After that, I'm leaving."

He was furious with me. "You needn't wait two weeks. The door's open now."

I started packing immediately. Grudgingly, Kirkpatrick said he would take me to the highway if I'd wait until he closed in the evening. "No, thanks. I'll go on and walk."

"How are you going to get way out there to the highway?"

"Well," I said, "it's only seven miles, and then I can catch the mail truck on into Gallup. The last I heard, walking wasn't all taken up." I started off and soon caught a ride to the Newcomb Post on Highway 666.

I told Mr. A. J. Newcomb that after three months and three days, I had quit Two Gray Hills. Newcomb was not surprised. "You've already stayed a month longer than any of Kirkpatrick's other help. No one wants to work for him because of the way he treats his employees."

When I finally got home that evening, I told Mother and Pop and anyone who cared to listen that I would never again work for anyone else! During the next few months, Pop, Bob, Malin and I toiled at getting Cousins Brothers in order. Later, Bob made a trip into Gallup and returned to say that the trader John Kirk wanted to see me about going to Chin Lee for some work. I was quick to say, "Absolutely not! I just left Two Gray Hills Post and promised myself I'd never take another job working for anyone else."

On the next trip into Gallup, I stopped by to see John Kirk. He asked me to take a job working for one of his friends, as a special favor. Well, Mr. Kirk was a smooth talker, and I needed money, so I finally agreed to go for two weeks to help him out of a pinch, but that was it. Two weeks. Next morning, Mother packed us a picnic lunch and my brother, Bob, and Aunt Lois and I took off in our 1932 Chevy pickup for Chin Lee.

When we got to the Thunderbird Trading Post and Guest Ranch at Chin Lee, it was closed. I went around back to the kitchen, where I was welcomed by the colored cook. She offered us lunch, but we declined and had our picnic on top of the mountain near there. My family then returned to Gallup, and the cook introduced herself as Mrs. Jackson and led me to one of the back rooms that was to be my bedroom. Mrs. Jackson then told me where to locate the owner, Mr. Cozy McSparron. He was attending a Navajo ceremonial dance, Yei Bi Chi, at the mouth of Canyon de Chelly. When I found Cozy, which wasn't hard, since he was the only one there who wasn't Navajo, I liked him immediately. He just handed me the keys to the post and said, "Go open up the store. I'll be there when I can." There were no preliminaries of any kind. He just trusted me right away.

Inside the post there was no cash register, only money in a drawer under the counter and cash everywhere along the back counter. In most trading posts, there were always six or eight inches of vacant space behind where the merchandise was displayed. This narrow ledge made a quick-change place and saved a lot of steps. In spare moments, it was collected and put in the drawer, and at the end of the day, cash sales were counted and written down.

That day, the post soon filled with Navajos who came to buy the usual general merchandise: flour, sugar, coffee, lard, canned fruit and vegetables, calico, and blankets. I found that nothing had prices marked. Later, Cozy just said, "You know what this stuff should sell for." And I guess I did.

We finally got down to talking business about my employment. Terms, living conditions, and wages were discussed and

Cozy McSparron, Bill Cousins, and Tugboat Annie, who set Bill up with his first date with Jean.

agreed upon. I would take my meals with the family in the dining room and had a private room and bath. The wages were princely, ninety dollars a month.

Part of my duties was to help with the "dudes," as Cozy called the tourists. The Thunderbird Guest Ranch had a Model A Ford four-door convertible, otherwise known as the "galloping showcase," that we used to take the guests for rides into Canyons de Chelly and del Muerto. The Ford had doughnut tires, which helped dig into the sand around the canyon. One of those "dudes" that I toured around was John D. Rockefeller. Somehow, Cozy was the custodian in charge of Canyon de Chelly. I think it was made legal by giving him a salary of a dollar a year.

A few miles into the canyon, the road forked, with del Muerto to the left and de Chelly straight ahead. Cozy charged fifteen dollars for a half-day trip, which went to Spider Rock in de Chelly. For thirty dollars, we took them into del Muerto as far as Massacre Cave and Mummy Cave, then back to the "Y" and into de Chelly up to Spider Rock. The full-day trip also included a picnic lunch.

Cozy was a great guy. I remember two young men who had spent the night at the ranch and took the all-day trip. When we got back, they couldn't pay their full bill. I called Cozy, and he said, "Just forget it. Tell them we were happy to have them as guests."

We closed the post about 5:00 PM every day and went to the house, where Cozy and I washed up, put on clean shirts, but no ties, and joined his wife, Inja, in their private sitting room. The first day I went in, Cozy already had a highball ready for us—moonshine mixed with pop. This was their evening tradition. Cozy said that when the business couldn't afford to buy our "moon," we would quit the business. It didn't take me very long to like the idea of having a drink every day before dinner.

Of course, any alcohol had be to smuggled in, just like it is today on the reservation. Carl and Wallace Gorman were two enterprising young men at Chin Lee who had trucks and did freighting for us and others in the area. They would make two or three trips a week when we needed anything, but didn't know that the items "special sugar" or "pottery" were moonshine. The shopkeeper who filled the order knew, though, and that's how we got our "shine." Later, we discovered that Carl and Wallace had a little business on the side hauling moonshine.

Cozy's wife, Inja, was a beautiful young woman from Kansas who was full of fun and very nice. She and Cozy had only been married a few months when I arrived. We always had dinner in the large combination living and dining room. There was a long table in the center and lots of comfortable chairs and couches all around the room. Often they had guests, and we always enjoyed good meals.

After I had been working for Cozy about six months, I got a letter from Bob saying he now had Cousins Brothers free from debt. This was music to my ears, and I wrote back that he could have my interest in the store, as I would be staying on at Thunderbird. My agreed-upon two weeks stretched into almost two years. Cozy was a fine person to work for and treated me like a member of the family. He changed my mind and shaped my ideas as to what a boss could be. We remained friends for many years.

I had been at Chin Lee working at the Thunderbird Post about a year when I met Jean. In May of 1934, she came home to Chin Lee from school in Flagstaff. I thought she was the prettiest girl I'd ever seen. By fall she would be my bride.

There was a scarcity of women in the area, but several lived and worked at a nearby boarding school. I would walk to the school almost every night, a mile at most, and visit with a very nice woman who was the cook, Gladys Emile. On the way, I had to walk past Dick Dunaway's house. Dick was Jean's stepfather and, even though I knew the family, I hadn't met Jean yet because she was away at school in Flagstaff.

Dick had a big German Shepherd dog that would growl and follow me, getting as close as twenty feet. Dick would stand out on his porch and laugh, thought it was real funny. Well, I had about enough of that damn dog. One evening, as I walked past the house, the dog started barking and running after me, as usual. Dick was standing on his porch, watching and laughing, having a hell of a good time.

"Hey, he's getting closer," I yelled at Dick.

"Yeah, he is," Dick agreed, grinning. I could tell Dick thought the world of that dog.

"Well," I warned, "I'm going to let him get just a little closer, then I'm going to kill him." I reached down into my pocket and pulled out a piece of three-quarter-inch galvanized pipe about two feet long that I carried with me. Dick called his dog off pretty quickly, and I never had any more problems with that shepherd.

The first time I saw Jean, she came into the Thunderbird store to buy a toothbrush. She was a beautiful little redhead, and I fell for her right away. I didn't know anything about love at first sight, but I knew that very day I wanted to marry her.

That summer, a dozen or so surveyors were hired by the National Park Service to make a topographic map of Canyon de Chelly and oversee the making of a trail down into the canyon at the White House lookout. They roomed at the Thunderbird Guest Ranch and were new to this part of the West. A couple of them were interested in Jean. One evening, after dinner, three or four of these fellows and I went out to the store to sit in the bull pen, drink soda pop, and shoot the breeze. One of them said, "I think I'll see if I can get a date with Jean tomorrow night."

I was standing behind the counter when he made this remark, and I just reached under the counter where we kept a loaded six-shooter, a Colt .45. I laid it on the counter top and said, "Damn it, leave her alone. She's mine." At that time, I hadn't even had the first date with her.

He quickly agreed. "All right, all right, all right!"

After that, I had no competition, but Jean couldn't figure out why these boys stopped their interest in her. After our marriage, I told her what happened. It's a good thing she thought it was all right by then.

A couple of nights after I first met Jean, I took Gladys to a dance at somebody's house. The surveyors all came, and everyone had a nice time. Jean's folks brought her; she was only eighteen. About ten o'clock, Jean said, "I have to go home. My parents will be expecting me."

I didn't want her walking home alone at that hour, so I told Gladys, "Let's go take Jean home."

Gladys was not happy with that idea. "No, you go ahead and take her home." I guess she was a little bit miffed, because after that, Gladys gave me a cold shoulder.

Tugboat Annie, the new cook at Thunderbird Ranch at Chin Lee, set me up with my first date with Jean to play tennis. I was too damn timid to ask her myself. Annie said, "I'll get you the date, but after that, you're on your own."

When I started going with Jean, I was on a high. Not too long after we started dating, I asked her to become my wife. Boy, when she accepted, I was walking ten feet tall!

I might say that Jean's parents were not overjoyed to lose her to me. Dick was not too fond of me after the dog incident, anyway, and thought I was a lazy Indian trader. One of their many arguments was that she smoked cigarettes. I told them I would buy them for her. In those days, all advertising led you to believe that they were good for you. Hell, I had smoked them since I was ten or twelve years old. Of course, this was something my parents didn't know. That smoking would become a huge problem many years later.

I wrote to my folks at the ranch that Jean and I were going to get married. My brother, Malin, was working as a trader at Frazier's Trading Store, twelve miles below Chin Lee, toward Kayenta. After he met Jean, he went out to the ranch to visit our folks.

Pop asked, "Have you met this girl that Bill's going to marry?"

"Yep," Malin answered.

"What does she look like?"

"She's red-haired and freckle-faced."

"Ugly as hell, huh?" my dad said with a laugh.

"Oh my God, no!" Malin said. "She's beautiful."

And she sure was.

Both Mother and Pop wrote me letters about the girl I had chosen to marry and our new life together:

Home Monday night, July 30th 1934

My dear darling Billie Boy:

Your letter reached me yesterday evening, and I was, as always, glad to hear from you, and while I have heard rumors, I still was surprised at the news your letter brought me. I hardly know just what I wish to say, but first of all, son, your happiness comes first with me. If this young lady is your choice, then she is mine too, and I am not in the least afraid that you would choose anyone beneath you. I wish I knew her, and am glad you're going to give us a chance to meet her. I'll have you a nice dinner and be looking for you.

I wish it was different with her religion but undoubtly her religion is her privilege and if you do not ask her to give hers up, then she won't ask you to give yours up. You must not think, my darling boy, that I won't feel bad to give you up, for I just can't help it. It's the breaking of the old home tie that brings the tears in spite of all. I shall say I have gained a daughter instead of lost a son but still I'll know there is to be a vacant place no one else will ever fill. I've missed you so much, seems you were so far away, and I have wished to come out there to see you but it was not to be. I hope you can come home occasionally. You know there will always be room at any time for you both. I believe you father feels just as I do on this subject. We all want you to be happy.

I wish I was able to help you a lot to get started to house-keeping—but anyway I will help all I can with my little "mite." And now darling boy I must go to bed for Rob is timekeeper for the new school work and we have to get up early. Howard will take the truck and bring us a load tomorrow. Rob bought a new one Sat. just like Malin was driving. Maybe he didn't want me to tell you might have been a "see-crat"— anyway I've told. I'll be looking and waiting for you and may God's richest blessing rest upon you both thro life, is the prayer of

Your Mother

Good night

— ~

My Darling Son:
What Mother has said, I say. If that is the girl you want that is the girl I want you to have, and I want you boath to remember that as long as pop and mother are alive our home is yours and hers and our home is open day and night for you boath. God bless you boath with our love to you boath from us all.

Pop

In 1934, Jean and I married in St. Michaels, Arizona. Right after the ceremony we all went to Gallup, where Cordie, Jean's mother, wanted us to have a wedding picture made. Then we went to a cafe and had something to eat and went grocery shopping. Cordie did the actual shopping, because we thought we could live on love. One item she bought was toilet paper, and we sure wouldn't have gotten that.

Late in the afternoon, we started for what we were to call home at Chin Lee. As luck would have it, we had a flat tire before we got there. I had to take the tire off the rim, patch the inner tube, then remount the tire and pump it up by hand. Since it was dark by then, we had to twist the toilet paper into little flares and burn it in order to see, lighting a little bit at a time from the roll.

We finally arrived in Chin Lee about 10 PM and took Cordie home, then went to ours. I drove with the headlamps off, because I was sure some of our friends were going to shivaree us. We got to our place and unloaded the groceries, then went in and turned the gas lantern off and waited in the dark for some time to be sure they would not shivaree us that night. They didn't come with their clanging noise until the next night.

After Jean and I married, Cozy let us live rent free in a big old house he owned. We only used the kitchen, one bedroom, and the living/dining room but the little bit of furniture our folks gave us sure looked lost in those big rooms.

Cozy gave me a raise when we got married, but it was still inadequate for us to live on. He offered to furnish our wood for heating and cooking, but I caught a certain look of disapproval on Inja's face. I think she wanted a single man working there, perhaps because some of the dudes had daughters with them. Anyhow, I didn't want to stay with things like that, so I thanked Cozy for everything. "I think it's time to move on."

Before I left Cozy's, a guest, Mrs. Harold Ickes, offered to help me get a job through her husband, who was Secretary of the Interior under F.D.R. Meantime, Jean became very sick, and I took her out to my folks at the ranch to recuperate. A government doctor diagnosed her with quinsy, but she really had scarlet fever. She was able to pass this on to several members of my family. I decided to leave Chin Lee and return to the ranch, too.

A few months later, I received a letter from the U.S. Indian Service telling me that I had a job at the U.S.I.S. warehouse in Gallup. The same day I received this job offer, I ran into the wholesaler, Mr. John Kirk, the same one who asked me to work for Cozy at Chin Lee a couple of years earlier. He asked me to take over the trading post at Borrego Pass. That seemed to be a promising thing to do.

Borrego Pass Post

Mike and John Kirk were traders in the Gallup area for many years. The Kirk Brothers Mercantile Company in Gallup supplied traders across the Navajo reservation. Here we see how John worked his below-market dealings, making a profit for the trader practically impossible.

Living at Borrego (Spanish for "sheep") Pass was difficult at best for the Cousinses. Imagine trying to maintain a clean home with no running water and riding over rough roads while in labor as Jean did. The Borrego Pass Post still functions today.

In 1933, the federal government began what it called the stock reduction program, designed to reduce the proliferation of livestock on overgrazed land on the Navajo reservation. Thousands of animals were slaughtered, leaving many Navajo families destitute and with no way to earn a living. The program was controversial and divisional. While his family was not deeply involved, Bill's view of the whole system, "there must have been a better way," seems to reflect the view of many.

Quest for Fortune

After a convalescent period for me and no work for Bill, he was offered a job working for John Kirk, who had been an Indian trader for many years. Bill had always thought Kirk was a pretty decent fellow, so we were an unsuspecting young couple who, one fine April day in 1935, moved to Borrego Pass to run the store for John Kirk.

We soon realized that he controlled the buying and selling of merchandise by below-market dealing. Borrego Pass was in the northwest part of New Mexico, near old Highway 66 and not too far from the Haspah oil fields. It was located between Crownpoint and Grants and Ambrosia Lake, in the area where they later discovered large uranium fields.

The trading post was on homestead land; therefore, it could not be taken from a homesteader. The Harveys, who were the original homesteaders, were so deeply indebted to Kirk, there was no hope for their financial recovery. They finally ended by turning their homestead over to Kirk in exchange for the debt they owed.

Kirk obtained part ownership of several posts in this way by extending credit to the traders. His prices were like extortion. They were almost always under market for wool, pelts, lamb rugs, and, in some years, piñon nuts. These traders didn't have money to buy from the competitors, thus getting in deeper and deeper with Kirk. All the while, Kirk was the spider looking for another to catch in his web.

Borrego Post, circa 1935. Below: Jean at Borrego Post, 1935.

The only good thing about that post was that the living quarters were connected to the store by a small wareroom or storage room. Never had I seen such a dilapidated, dirty place. The homesteader, Mrs. Harvey, was a cat lover, and the entire house reeked of cats. Plus there was no running water. We had not been there more than a couple of days when I remarked to Bill how dirty and smelly it was. Mrs. Harvey heard me from the other side of the room and answered sharply, "You try living here twenty or thirty years with no water and see how clean you keep it!"

The water at the Borrego Post came from a seepage spring, a "hot weather spring," which produced water only in the summer time. This spring was located up a rocky hill and yielded a couple of ten-quart buckets every twenty-four hours. Bill built himself a yoke to carry two five-gallon buckets of water in each trip.

This strange water could only be used for drinking, because any food cooked in the spring water turned black. Potatoes and beans could simmer all day and would still be hard. At first, it tasted terrible, but after about ten days, a person got used to it, and no other water satisfied our taste. And it was the strongest physic any of us ever had!

There was also a large cistern to catch rainwater when and if it rained. That was used for laundry and various cleaning jobs. Our cooking water, and all our water in the winter, was hauled in fifty-gallon drums from Thoreau, a small settlement on old Highway 66 about twenty or thirty miles away.

In the late thirties and early forties, the uranium fields were developed near this old Borrego Post. Bill and I always thought we had received dangerous exposure to hazardous material, but now we are in our seventies and eighties, with no cancer. Who knows?

I was very much pregnant by then, and the baby chose this time to arrive. My mother and Bill's were with us for the big event, so, fearing the worst, we grabbed a string and some scissors and off we went to the hospital. Wouldn't you know we ran off the old, muddy road and got stuck! I think Bill practically lifted that car back on track. We made it in time to Rehoboth, New Mexico, where Edward was born on August 4, 1935.

Greenhorn parents Jean and Bill with new baby, Edward.

If ever there was a pair of "greenhorn parents," it was us. What we didn't know about parenting, though, was made up in love. Edward was the first and, as it turned out, the only

In the unforgettable winter of 1937, Bill and his friends shoveled eight miles of section line road from Cousins Brothers to the highway so they could get supplies.

grandson from the Cousins brothers as well as my side of the family.

Sometime before we left Borrego's Pass, I got the mumps. We had gone swimming in a Zuni water tank, and one of the farmer's daughters who was playing around in the water had the mumps. Before it was over, Bill, his brother Bob's wife, Betty, and his mother all caught the mumps. It was very tough on the adults.

We stayed at Borrego until January of 1937, when Mr. Kirk sold the post to another trader. After almost two years, we left Borrego Pass around mid-January. We had no job nor money but were undaunted in our quest for fortune, if not fame.

We headed back to the Cousins homeplace to regroup and make plans. It was a winter to remember. Every morning we got up to a new snow, enough to keep us inside fussing at the weatherman and each other. That year we did a lot of reading, for the Cousins family had a wonderful library. Bill and his brother, Bob, with a group of Navajo men, shoveled the eight miles of section line road up to State Road 32, locally known as the Zuni Highway. There the eldest brother, Tom, would meet Bob and Bill with the mail and a few groceries. More than one of these trips to the highway was made by horse-drawn sleigh. Fortunately, we were all in good health that winter.

Working for John Kirk

When Jean and I had been married less than a year, we moved to the Borrego Pass Trading Post, which I managed for the wholesaler, Mr. John Kirk. Borrego Post was located approximately fifty miles northeast of Gallup. We had very little water. The only water we had, other than what we hauled from Thoreau, New Mexico, was from a tunnel dug into the side of a hill, under a large cliff of rocks. The tunnel went about thirty feet into the hill, like a mineshaft, about five feet wide and six feet high. The entire tunnel was made of clay. Water dripped from the clay ceiling a drop at a time and fell to the hard-packed clay floor, where there were little troughs cut into the floor that ran down into a ten-gallon galvanized tank buried in the ground. For some reason, the hotter and drier the weather, the more water it produced.

In the winter and during the rainy season, we didn't get much water. The sides and ceiling of the tunnel were covered with a yellow substance which I thought was sulfur. Now I feel sure it was uranium salts, because, in later years, we found that most all of that country was rich in uranium. In fact, it was very close to the place where United Nuclear had their big uranium ore mine.

Jean and I had been married a little over ten months when our son, Edward, was born, August 4, 1935. When the doctor told us, "The baby could come any day now; better stay close to Gallup," we went to stay with my family at Cousins Brothers.

This put us closer to the hospital at Rehoboth, which was located about six miles east of Gallup. At 2:00 in the morning of August 4, we realized that it was time for Jean to go to the hospital. We had quite a caravan. I drove Jean, her mother, and mine. We'd had several days of rains, so my brother, Bob, and a friend, Howard Wirtz, followed in their cars in case we had car trouble or bad roads.

When we came to "twelve mile hill," so called because it was twelve miles from Gallup, we found the road washed out and a ditch running across the highway that was about two feet wide and four feet deep. I knew that the right wheels would have to cross that ditch. After looking it over, I figured the best way would be to jump the car across the ditch. I told everybody to hold on tight, backed up a ways, and took a run at it. We bounced right across. We arrived at the hospital in Rehoboth in plenty of time, because the baby didn't make his appearance until 7:00 AM. Edward was not only our pride and joy, but for both our families, he was the first grandchild.

Later, I called the hospital office and they told me that the hospital bill would be ninety dollars for the ten-day stay for mother and baby. I said, "No problem. I'll have the money for you tomorrow." Of course, I didn't have that much money. So, I went to the bank and asked to borrow seventy-five for sixty days.

The banker said, "Bill, we can't loan it to you unless John Kirk signs the note. Mr. Kirk left instructions for the bank not to loan you any money unless he signed for it."

"Get the note ready, and I'll take it to him," I said.

When I handed Kirk the note, he said, "Hell, I wouldn't even sign a note for my brother."

"No," I said, furious with his attitude. "But you'll sign this one."

"Now, why would I do that?"

"You had no damn business cutting my credit off, and you know you won't have to pay it back." Well, he signed the note and I got my money. Within the sixty days, I had paid the bank back, just as I said I would do. I should have known then that I wouldn't last long with John Kirk.

The trouble with working for Kirk was that he owned the wholesale house where I had to buy my goods and merchandise, and he charged me just 10 percent under the retail price. He would knock down the prices he paid me for the rugs, wool, and lambs that I bought from my customers, the Navajos, who lived nearby. My deal with him was for a salary of ninety dollars a month, which was barely enough to cover the groceries, plus 40 percent of the net profits. Of course, he made sure there was never a net profit. I never would have agreed to his deals if Ayn Rand had written the book *Atlas Shrugged* and I had read it then.

One day, two of Kirk's sons came out to the post from Gallup. That fall, I had purchased approximately two tons of piñon nuts from my customers. The boys wanted me to bring the nuts into town right away as they were trying to fill a carload to ship. I asked them, "How much is Mr. Kirk paying?"

"Five cents a pound," they said.

"That's no good," I said. "I'm sure I could get double that or better."

"Just bring them into town."

The next day, I loaded the piñons onto my truck and started to Gallup. I happened to stop at Jones Mercantile in Thoreau, which was also the post office where I received my mail. Mr. Jones asked. "Bill, what have you got on your truck?"

"A new crop of piñons," I answered.

"Hey, I'll give you thirteen cents a pound for them."

"Sold!" Heck, I quickly unloaded those piñons for him and headed on into Gallup, taking the check to Mr. Kirk. He was very happy to see me, thinking he was going to get the piñons. I asked him again about the price.

He said, "A nickel a pound."

I gave him the check along with the weight slip. "We both made money on this, Mr. Kirk."

He was furious that I had sold them for more money to someone else. Right then, I saw the handwriting on the wall. And, sure enough, he sold the place right out from under me when we had been there a little less than two years.

At Borrego, we sacked the wool we bought from the Indians. At every trading post, the traders had what we called a wool rack. It was made of two-by-fours and two-by-sixes, about seven feet high and approximately 3 1/2 feet square, with a thirty-six-inch round hole at the top. We had an iron ring made out of 1/2 inches or 5/8 inches rod and welded together. This ring was just a little larger than the hole in top of the wool rack. You would fold the wool sack over the ring and pin it there with spike nails. We would put the wool in this sack, which was about 6 1/2 feet long, a little at a time; then you would climb down into the sack and stomp on it to pack it down. Generally we got a little better than two hundred pounds per sack. Some of the wool sackers could pack it so tightly that they would get nearly three hundred pounds to the sack of wool.

The small living quarters at Borrego consisted of a kitchen and a bedroom. Fortunately the bedroom was large enough to have a few comfortable chairs in there beside the bed, so that was also our living room.

The people who had owned the post before we were there had moved everything out of the house and stored it in a shed in the back yard. The only thing they hadn't moved out was a baby grand piano. We needed the room, so after about a month of waiting for them to come for the piano, we decided

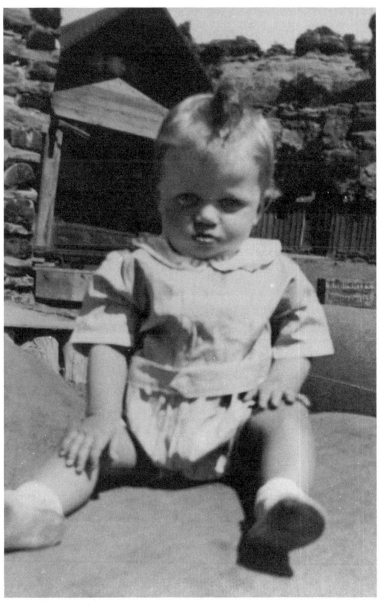

Edward sitting on a sack of wool at Borrego Post, circa 1936.

to move it ourselves. We hired two or three Navajos to help. One was Paddy Martinez, who later discovered uranium at Tent Mountain, not far from where we lived. As we were struggling to move this huge piano, Paddy said, "Next time, Bill, why don't you just buy a fiddle."

A few days later a man of about sixty-five years came out from Reidling Music Company in Albuquerque to repossess the piano, since no payments had been made in a long time. He tried, without luck, to sell the piano to me. It just happened that my brother, Bob, and his wife, Betty, had come out that day for a visit. They decided to buy the piano. The man from Reidling Music happily said he would deliver it to them at Cousins Brothers. The old guy amazed us by refusing any help in moving that huge piano. We were completely surprised when he dismantled the whole thing, took it apart into small pieces, and moved it all by himself.

When we had been at Borrego less than two years, one day in early December, Vernon Bloomfield, son of trader George Bloomfield, came to the post with a letter from Kirk stating that he had bought the post and would take over right away. He asked me to vacate. Just like that. A friend, Van Muncy, and I started moving out all our personal possessions in a snow storm that dumped about sixteen inches on the ground. We stored some things in a warehouse in Thoreau, and Jean and I and the new baby headed for the ranch at Cousins Brothers to live with my folks until I could find something else.

I suppose no story about working with the Navajo people in the 1930s would be complete without a word about the stock reduction program. It started in 1933 as a way to reduce overgrazing and soil erosion. What it did was to pauperize a lot of Navajo families. There isn't much good to say about it, and I'm not even sure it achieved its purpose of improving the land. One true result was that the Indians, and most traders, ended up hating John Collier, who was the commissioner of Indian affairs.

I was only involved in sheep reduction, but I know that horses and goats had to go, too. At Chin Lee, the traders were told by the government to buy sheep from the Navajo. We had to go out to the corral and "mouth" all the sheep, that is, check their teeth so we could write down their ages. We would brand them with paint, go back to the store and pay the Indians for the sheep, around four to five dollars a head. Later, the Indian Service would reimburse us for the amount. But we were never paid for our part of the work. After the sheep were bought, the Navajos could butcher any they wanted, whether they were the original owners or not. But they had to leave the pelt with us to turn in to the government.

The Navajos realized this was taking their livelihood, and none wanted to get rid of their livestock. Many went broke and hungry during those years.

Later, to show what a good job they had done, the Indian Service fenced off sections of land here and there with a six-strand barbed wire fence around it and called these "demonstration areas." Nothing was allowed to graze inside these areas. I only saw one, approximately ten miles north of Wide Ruins near Klagetoh. This particular "demonstration area" didn't prove anything. There was no grass on either side of the fence. I asked some of the older Indians about this, and they explained that there was no grass inside because the hooves of the sheep planted the grass seed as they moved around while grazing. There was generally enough grass after spring rains. Trouble was, we didn't always get the rain we needed.

I'm sure there were parts of the reservation that were overgrazed. But there must have been a better way to fix the problem than the stock reduction plan.

Most traders used trade tokens, or *seco*, at one time. The Navajos called them Paish-ti-ee, meaning "thin metal." They were made of brass or aluminum, and on the token were printed the words, "Good in Trade 50 ¢" or "25 ¢," all the way to "$5.00." The traders used them to make sure they were paid back for pawn. If you gave cash for pawned items, it might take the trader one to several years to receive cash payment on pawn. And the trader couldn't charge tax on the reservation. The tokens ensured they would return to trade. We also gave out due bills, written notes that said, "Due bearer ten dollars in trade." Later they were declared illegal, and those tokens became big for collectors.

My dad's tokens were especially in demand because they were made of brass and octagon shaped. When I was young, he decided to quit using them. He burned them, then dug a hole several feet deep and buried them. I suppose they are still out there somewhere in the 160 acres that was Cousins, New Mexico. Since there is nothing left of the buildings, they probably won't ever be found.

God's Little Acre

Bill's "spinster aunt," as Jean calls her, was a career woman, poet, and fine teacher who became New Mexico's first female state school superintendent. Lois Randolph traveled from Oklahoma to visit her sister, Lucie, who had married Charles Cousins and moved to Indian country. Lois fell in love with the Southwest and decided to stay. One of her first jobs was to try to tame and educate the four rowdy Cousins boys. That accomplished, she moved on to larger schoolrooms but remained a dedicated and influential family member.

The first items the Indians created specifically for trade were crude beaded trinkets, but as their popularity with tourists grew, the variety, quality, and art of such articles also increased. We see a progression of this improvement over the years from the early, remote posts to Jean's competitive business in Gallup.

The heartbreak of losing their own business and home at the hopeful "God's Little Acre" must have been great, yet both Jean and Bill temper their stories with humor and optimism. It's interesting to note that Jean was not included in the actual negotiations of the move to Wide Ruins. Even though she, like most traders wives, worked with Bill at all of the posts, she was never paid a separate salary until much later, when she became employed by another business in Gallup.

Bill and Sallie Lippincott, who took over ownership of the Wide Ruins Post, are credited with the renewal of the old-time vegetal-dyed Navajo rugs and a general improvement in the quality of the weaving at that time. Their friends, Cozy and Inja McSparron, also encouraged Chin Lee weavers to use natural dyes, and many of the old Chin Lee rugs show that style and dye method. We can see how these two couples influenced this beautiful art form and the roles Jean and Bill Cousins played in accomplishing a quality finished product.

Working Toward a Dream

Bill's spinster Aunt Lois homesteaded a section of land about fifteen miles as the crow flies south and east of the ranch, the Cousins home. She told us that if Bill and I would start a little trading post on her land, she would deed us forty acres. So, as soon as weather permitted, Bill and his brother Bob started cutting logs for a small store and a one-bedroom living quarters. They dug a well in the nearby arroyo. Bill used the yoke he had fashioned to fit over his shoulders at Borrego, carrying two five-gallon buckets at a time, to haul all the water needed for our house and Aunt Lois's.

In the late summer of 1937, the first building was completed. Bob's wife, Betty, and I tended Cousins Brothers while the men finished the house. Quite a few Navajos lived in the area, but our closest neighbor was a Navajo family, the Pintos, who lived a couple of miles away. "Old man Pinto," George, had two wives. His first wife was barren, so he took another. They both lived with him, and the second wife produced a whole cow pen full of children. Everybody worked together to take care of them, and it was all very agreeable.

Whenever Bill's father had to be away from home, "Old Man Pinto" always sent his wife, Bertha, to take care of Mother Cousins and keep her company. The two ladies didn't speak each other's languages, but they got along fine. Bill's mother had beautiful red curly hair, and folks called her "Mother

Cousins" as a mark of respect. But the name highly irritated her. "I'm not their mother," she would say. "Call me Lucie."

George and Bertha Pinto were great neighbors. Bertha had been educated. So had George, but he lapsed back into his native culture and seemed to forget everything he learned.

To the south of us was the Zuni farming village of Nutria. The Zunis were generally a nice people, and they had rich gardens and also raised quite a lot of wheat. From them we bought beaded rabbit feet and beaded faces on sheep or goat vertebrae for neckerchief or bandana slides. These were among our first trade items. There were not too many silversmiths in Zuni at that time, although Bob was working with a few who supplied Cousins Brothers.

The whole country was still depressed and would be until the early forties. Times were tough for everyone, and we were barely eking by, so we attempted to improve our income with a small chicken business. All we got out of that was lots of work, loss of sleep, and chasing coyotes.

A hogan was built for the chickens with a stove in the middle and, every two weeks, one hundred day-old baby chicks arrived. Bill set the alarm for every two hours to replenish the fire and unbunch the chicks. They are stupid creatures and huddle together so tightly they will smother if not prevented. This two-hour vigil went on for several weeks, or until they were fully feathered. Bill managed to raise one hundred of them and, by that time, a new bunch had arrived. When the first bunch was about ready for market, the coyotes discovered how tasty they were and had a few. We struggled with those chicks to make them profitable, but it was futile. We ate a lot of fried chicken that year.

Finally, as things got harder, Bill and Bob began to take a few construction jobs in town to get a few pennies. Bob and Betty were taking care of the ranch and Mom and Pop Cousins but still managed to come our way. What a loving, caring brother and sis they were.

Winters weren't especially bad while we were at God's Little Acre. During the summer rains and muddy roads, one couldn't get through except with horses or to walk. These were the worst of times as well as some wonderful times. Several Anglo bean farmers were scattered around the area, and we often got together for barn dances, birthdays, ball games, picnics, or anything that would give all of us some social contact and fun. The men, including some Navajo men who were very good ball players, had quite a baseball team, which was lots of fun along with a picnic lunch.

We all took our children along, for there were no babysitters in those days. When the little ones got tired, we wrapped them in a blanket or quilt and laid them on benches, the floor, or in the cool shade of a tree. We made our own fun, had time for reading and many a picnic meal of bacon and eggs or pinto beans and, once in a while, a dish of canned tomatoes under those beautiful tall pines.

The problems of store-keeping were numerous. That country was overrun with packrats, and they always left something in return, mostly twigs or pine cones. It seemed that no matter what Bill did, they kept coming. In those days we sold lots of dried fruit, peaches, prunes, and apricots. These came in wooden boxes and weighed from fifteen to twenty-five pounds. Those packrats loved that fruit, and it disappeared as if by magic—while the money did not increase. Months later, when Bill was chopping wood, he cut into a big log. When he finally got it split, the hollow center was full of dried fruit and beaded rabbit feet from our stock. Those darned packrats had been hard at work.

One Sunday, while all was quiet, I took our little son and walked down the short distance to visit Aunt Lois. Bill was reading at home when the rats came calling. We always kept a rifle hanging over the door between the living room and storeroom. There were a couple of rats having fun and Bill stood in the doorway and took aim at the one on the top shelf. The shot sort of ruined our stack of crystal wedding glasses and plates, but we had one less rat. Crystal wedding glassware came as gifts in oatmeal boxes, so it was cheap stuff.

Bill looked again and could just see the foot of the other rat. He aimed again and fired. Alarmed at the sounds of shots, Aunt Lois and I hurried up the hill to see what was going on. "Two down," said Bill proudly. But what a mess.

Sadly, in the early fall of 1938, we decided that the chicken business and the post at God's Little Acre weren't ways to make a living. And, as Bill predicted to the trader at Pine Haven, we were both going broke. He lasted only a little longer than we and settled for twenty-five cents on the dollar with his suppliers.

We had borrowed some cash from family members, less than a thousand dollars, and managed to pay it all back. Both our folks were coming regularly to check on us and always with a bag of groceries. We knew this was no place for a growing family to be.

In late August we were off to see my parents at Chin Lee, having received word that maybe there would be a job for Bill at one of the trading posts. While there, someone took a picture of Edward, who was about three. In the background was an old Indian man who lived nearby and was quite docile. When Pop Cousins saw that picture, he became extremely upset. He recognized the man in the photo as Blackman (Hosteen Klijinni), one of the Navajos involved in the incident at Chin Lee who robbed the post and came back to flaunt the jewelry he claimed he won gambling. Pop Cousins was locked inside the post with him all day long, so we figured he knew

Edward with Blackman at Chin Lee.

the man. He certainly didn't want his young grandson so close to a man he considered a thief and dangerous.

Bill's old employer from Thunderbird Post, Cozy McSparron, knew of a young couple who was fresh out of college and eager to have a trading post. But they needed help in learning how to manage it. It took about a month of negotiations before we could accept their offer. Meantime, Bill had agreed to work for Camillo Garcia at the Garcia store in Chin Lee during September at a handsome wage for those days. Finally, arrangements were made for us to go to this place called Kin Teel, meaning "wide house," by the Navajo people, and Wide Ruins by the white man.

The post had been owned by Peter Parquette, one of the first Indian agents at Fort Defiance, and my husband, Bill, helped with the inventory on the day of purchase. Since Bill spoke the Navajo language very well, he was valuable in dealing with the Indians. They were concerned about what would happen with their pawn and came to the post in a large, loud group. Bill convinced the new owner that it would create good relations with their future customers to keep the pawn, even though it wasn't very profitable. The property of the Wide Ruins Post had been gradually surrounded by the Navajo reservation, and several Indian families lived there, so friendly relationships had to be established to make the post successful.

The new owners, Bill and Sallie Lippincott, wanted us to come and work for them in their new enterprise. The job was to last one year while Bill taught them the trading business. Ha! We were there for thirteen years in all.

How we hated to leave our little log cabin, but in October of 1938, we began making preparations to move out of God's Little Acre. It wasn't too long afterward that even Aunt Lois went to the Cousins family ranch to live. We moved on to Wide Ruins.

Everything but Trade

Jean and I made arrangements with Aunt Lois to buy forty acres from her homesteaded 640 acres about twelve miles from the ranch. Against Pop's advice, we decided to put up a trading post there. I generally took his advice, but this time I didn't and regretted it later. Bob helped me cut logs and build a store and living quarters out of the logs. It was a comfortable and beautiful place, with lots of large pine trees on the property. One of the things I liked most about what we called God's Little Acre was the quietness. I always thought it was the quietest place I had ever been. The only thing you could hear was birds singing or coyotes howling. Once in a while, late in the evenings, way off in the distance, you could hear a Navajo singing as he rode along home.

Our first problem was no water. I tried to rectify that problem by digging the well myself. At twenty-five feet, I hit solid sandstone. Using dynamite, I blasted down to thirty-five feet, but it seemed that the deeper I went, the drier it got. Finally, I gave up and carried our water from the well in the canyon. And I had to shovel all the dirt back into that hole to fill it up.

To augment our income, I went out in the woods and cut sprags while Jean ran the store. Sprags were made from scrub oaks, cut 2 1/2 to 3 inches thick by 24 inches long, with the bark peeled and the ends pointed. I hauled about three thousand sprags at a time, and it took me two to three months to get a load that size. We sold these sprags to a coal mine near Gallup for around six or eight cents each, so there wasn't much money to be made that way. The sprags were used as brakes for coal cars down in the mine. When the miners wanted to stop the car, they would throw a sprag into the spokes of the wheels.

God's Little Acre was located on the edge of the Zuni reservation, so we got some Zuni trade. Mostly we bought beaded rabbit's feet and cow heads. The rabbit's feet were just beadwork around a dried rabbit's foot. People would buy them for good luck charms. The cow heads were made from the vertebrae of sheep. These were used to hold a bandana around a person's neck.

One day a man came to the store and introduced himself as H.C. Smith. "I'm going to put in a large trading post down the way at Pine Haven," he claimed.

"Well, that's bad news for me, as most of my customers have to come right by there to get to my post," I said. Pine Haven was about three miles from us.

"I'm sorry," he said. "But those are my plans."

"I'm sorry, too," I answered. "Because these people around here are poor, and I don't think their trade will be enough to keep us both going." That proved to be right, because later we both went broke.

After God's Little Acre, we went back to Chin Lee, where I found a job working at the Garcia Trading Post. Mr. Garcia was a good man to work for, paying fairly nice wages for those days, about ninety-five dollars a month. My jobs included buying lambs for him and trading in the store. We lived with Jean's folks, Cordie and Dick, during that time.

Cozy asked me to meet and talk with this young couple who was buying the Wide Ruins Trading Post and would surely be hiring someone. I wanted to make a good impression, so I

Jean, young Edward, and Bill, well-suited for the job at Wide Ruins.

put on my only suit, a white shirt, and a tie—pink, as I recall—and went to Gallup to meet them. Bill and Sallie Lippincott walked in, both dressed in cowboy duds of Levis, western shirts, cowboy boots, and ten-gallon hats. I don't know what kind of impression I made, but they offered me a job. There were a few problems with it, though. The job didn't start for five weeks and was only to last six months, long enough for them to learn the business (they thought!). I didn't like the way the salary was offered, which was to furnish my groceries as part of the deal. I wanted them to pay me wages, and I'd buy my own groceries. The Lippincotts wanted me to give them an answer by the end of the month, and we agreed to meet at Cozy's in Chin Lee.

Meantime, I continued working for Mr. Camillo Garcia. He knew that I would possibly stay only a month. In my favor, I knew that Mr. Garcia wanted me to stay on working with him, and I wouldn't have minded that at all. He was a fine man to work for. I told him, "I'll probably stay, because I'm going to make an offer that I don't think Lippincott will agree with. But I've already committed myself to giving him an opportunity. I'll go down to Cozy's and straighten out this wage thing." Both of us thought I'd end up at Garcia's.

I went down to Cozy's that night to talk with the Lippincotts. We all sat in the living room: Cozy and Inja, Bill and Sallie Lippincott. I said, "I want to be paid a retaining fee for the month that I didn't work." Now, a month's wage was a lot of money in those days, about ninety-five dollars, and I knew they were not going to pay me, because we'd already argued over the wages. But I held firm. "I want a salary, not to include groceries. And I want my contract to be at least a year, not six months." I didn't want to move my family around like that, and six months isn't enough for anything in the trading business. I knew I was pushing it, but I figured my ace card was that I could keep working for Garcia.

Lippincott turned around to Cozy. "What do you think? He's asking a lot."

Cozy said, "I would advise you to take his offer."

Lippincott turned to his wife. "Sallie, bring me my checkbook." Without another argument, he wrote me a check for the month I didn't work for them. He agreed to everything I had asked for—retainer, salary, and a year's contract.

All along, I figured I was going to have to leave Wide Ruins after a year. I thought I probably could get a job at a trading post somewhere, maybe even back to Garcia's. A fellow who could speak the Navajo language and knew the trading business was always in demand and could find a job. But there was a lot of talk about California, and I thought about going out there to look for work.

On the morning the Lippincotts were to take over the Kin Teel Post at Wide Ruins, I was there early, before anyone, to help with the inventory and sale.

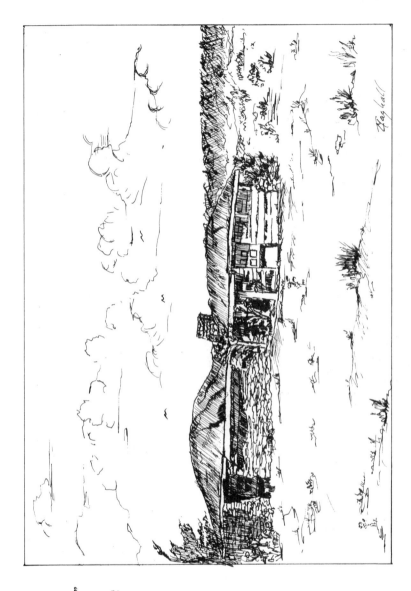

*Rare double hogans
provided a spacious
home "full of centipedes"
for the Cousins family
during their first year at
Wide Ruins in 1938.*

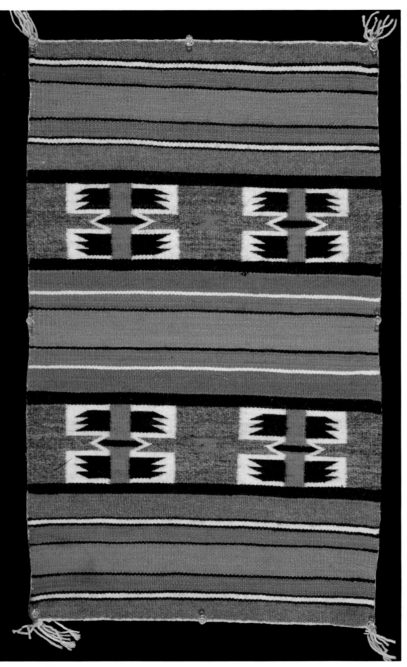

1950s Wide Ruins rug woven by Louise Dale, one of the first weavers in the Wide Ruins area to make a vegetal-dye rug. Typical Wide Ruins squash blossom design using all-vegetal dye colors.

Photo made after the wedding of Jean and Bill Cousins on September 10, 1934.

Aerial view of Wide Ruins Post in its heyday.

Jean with Navajo customers at Wide Ruins Post, circa 1945.

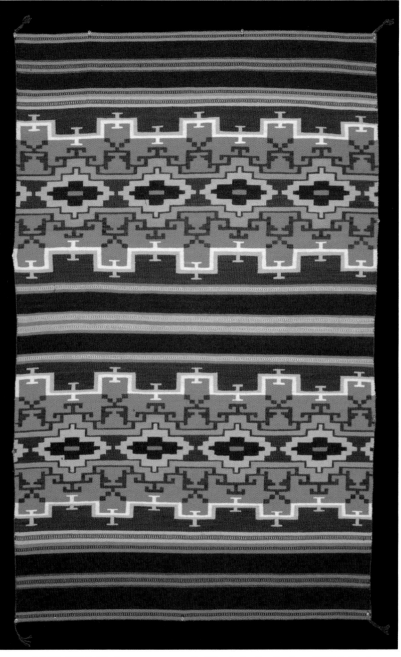

*1960s Wide Ruins rug woven by Virginia Ambroise of Wide Ruins.
Squash blossom design elaborately stylized.*

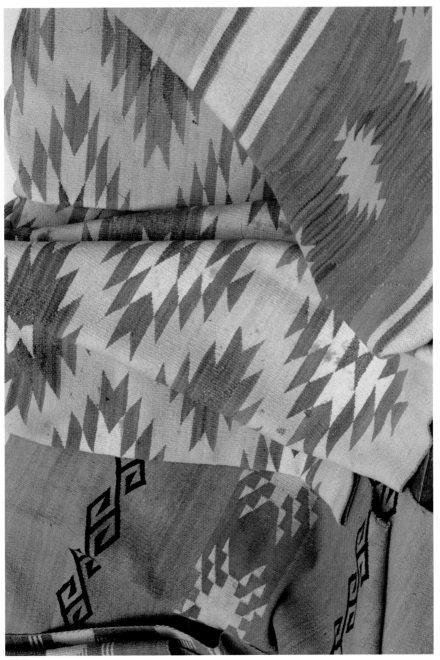

Group of 1940s Wide Ruins rugs, vegetal dye, courtesy Morning Star Traders, Tucson, AZ.

Top side (heads) of trade tokens (seco) from C. C. Cousins General Merchandise (Pop Cousin's store at Whitewater) and Wide Ruins Trading Post. Below: Flip side (tails) of trade tokens from Cousins and Wide Ruins.

Jean and Bill in buggy, just before retirement.

Watercolor of
Wide Ruins Post by
Sally Freund.

Wide Ruins

Jean's main interests during this period were her home and growing family, but she continued to help in the post. As always, she points out the small pleasures of her life. The artist Jimmy Toddy—Beatien Yazz—still lives in the Navajo community of Wide Ruins today, and several of his children are artists of merit.

Bill's business acumen and relationships with the Navajos are revealed as he finally finds an employer who trusts him enough to allow him to develop a thriving business at the post. The relationship between Bill Cousins and Bill Lippincott was one of mutual friendship and respect, which allowed both to excel. Bill's methods of dealing with the problems and solutions of World War II rationing stamps prove his innovation and integrity. And then there is the issue of pride, when times were toughest and Bill couldn't get a job to support his family. Rather than work for the man who laughed at him, Bill showed his independent spirit by walking away. Years later, he was strong enough to compliment Mr. Hine and call him a friend.

Ason Chee

Our new employers, Bill and Sallie Lippincott, must have been amazed to see us arriving at Wide Ruins with our pickup load of belongings. We certainly were shocked when we discovered our quarters were a couple of quite spacious hogans on top of the hill just above the Wide Ruins post. At that time, some of the original ruins walls of the old Indian ruins were still standing next to our hogans.

The hogans had been repaired to an extent that floors were installed and the roof fixed, but never in my life had I lived in a place so full of centipedes. Again, Bill had to carry our water up the hill from the spring at the store. And once again we used gasoline lanterns for light and a chemical toilet outside. It wasn't too bad, but certainly not very good.

These hogans were snug and warm, with only a small cookstove for heat in the kitchen area. One discouraging thing was, it seemed that every time I started to cook or we sat down to eat, a little stream of sand would come trickling down on the food.

We did a lot of reading that winter, for we couldn't afford a radio and after we had settled in, Bill sold our equity in our pickup to pay off some of the bills. Hence, we were afoot. Thank goodness we were still healthy.

I learned to do more things with canned corned beef and other canned meats than Heinz could do with a pickle. Only rarely did we have fresh meat and few fresh vegetables. There

Jean standing beside double hogans in which they lived when they moved to Wide Ruins, 1938.

Hosteen Glish, who worked at the post, Jean, Bill Cousins (in his classic stance), and Sallie Lippincott.

was no way to keep them, since we had no electricity and no refrigeration in the hogan.

But things were getting better. Bill and I felt that since we had made it through the last three tough years, we could handle anything. Before we knew it, our agreed-upon year at Wide Ruins was drawing to a close. The Lippincotts seemed to have plenty of money and were gone a lot. Around August, Bill Lippincott asked us if we would stay on. We had a few conditions. We were tired of living in the hogans with no lights or water or plumbing. If they would build us a small, modern house, we would stay. They agreed.

That being settled, work began almost at once on the Little House. To us, it was a palace and our first modern home. We also had a pay increase, and our debts began dwindling. Thinking that we could handle small car payments, Bill found us a Chevy. What a thrill to ride again! Our trips in cars had been few and far between.

Damage to the outside of Wide Ruins after the hi-life explosion.

Did I tell you about the explosion at Wide Ruins? What excitement! And what a mess!

Any housewife or grocery storekeeper knows about weevils. They are to flour, cereals, and cornmeal what moths are to wool—devastating! Those minute creatures were ensconced in one of the warerooms, and the decision was made to extinguish them by using a chemical, carbon disulfide, commonly known as "hi-life." As a gas, it was supposed to evaporate and kill all the weevils.

On Saturday evening at closing time, Bill and another manager, J. B. Fordyce, sealed all doors and windows with tape. All gas and refrigerants were shut off, and open cans of the chemical were distributed in the warerooms and storeroom. Then the last outside door was sealed as they left.

Before we could walk up the hill to our home, it blew up with a boom and a roar. We all turned in time to see the store roof and assorted merchandise pitched about ten feet in midair. Then the roof settled back in its place, pinning shovels, saddles, bridles, ropes, and other items that had been

Destruction and mess inside Wide Ruins after the hi-life explosion.

hanging from the ceiling between the roof and walls. It was sure a strange sight. Little fires sparked everywhere. Bill and J. B. used small, hand-held fire extinguishers to put it out and finally finished the job with the water hose. Then we went inside to view the damage.

The place was a mess. The glass showcases were broken, and shards were everywhere. The acrid smell was horrible. Flour and cornmeal covered everything like snow. The phone was blown off the wall but still worked, so we could call to report the accident.

Since no one was quite sure about insurance coverage, J. B. advised Bill not to say there had been an explosion. In a few days, an insurance adjuster came from Flagstaff and began questioning J. B. Not satisfied with the answers, he turned to Bill and asked, "What the hell exploded? I know there's been an explosion with this kind of mess."

Bill was tight-lipped. "I was instructed not to tell."

The adjuster made a phone call to the office and reported that the post was fully covered with insurance. Then, the full story was revealed. The insurance man just shook his head and chuckled as he listened. "Hi-life'll do it, all right."

In the fall of 1939, Bill's father, "Pop" Charles Cousins, became desperately ill with heart problems. He died in May of 1940 and was buried in National Cemetery in Santa Fe.

Both Bill and his father spoke the Navajo language, but I only learned a few words, enough to get by. I knew that there was one word that would do for sardines, hay, and rope. The Indians gave us Navajo names. I was Ason Chee, meaning "red-haired woman." Bill, who towered over everyone, was called Hosteen Nez, meaning "tall man."

My most embarrassing moment involved trying to speak the difficult Navajo language. Sis is a sack in Navajo; sizz is a penis.

And I got them mixed up. Boy did I get myself into trouble! I was the laughing stock of the Wide Ruins community. So that ended my use of the word. I didn't even try; I just asked the customers if they wanted a paper to put their purchases in.

The Indians kept telling Bill that there was a rattlesnake den not too far from the store, and our home was certainly in the path of their migration. In the spring and fall, that place was lousy with rattlesnakes, sidewinders, and bullsnakes. Now, the Navajo would not kill one unless it was a life and death situation. They believed that snakes were a connection to the netherworld. But I didn't share that belief.

While we were living at the Little House, I killed my first snake. Our son, Edward, not quite five years old, was out in the yard playing while I was raking and cleaning the front yard of building debris. In the wood scraps, I unearthed a huge rattlesnake. He coiled up and rattled at me just as I chopped him in two. Afterward I got scared of our close call and made Edward come inside with me while I calmed down. Later, Bill went out and found a bunch of snakes, all coiled up together, having a sun bath near some rocks where they denned. He took his twelve-gauge shotgun and disposed of them. It was just too unsafe for us to live so close to them.

Jimmy Toddy (pronounced "toe-dee"), young son of Joe Toddy, who worked around the post, had a great talent for drawing. His family, which included his father, Joe, and grandmother, Little Woman, lived near the Wide Ruins post. The Lippincotts recognized his talent at a young age and took him under their wing. They bought supplies and furnished him a place to paint. Sallie acted as his sponsor and eventually sold his paintings and invested the money for him. He was very productive and signed his work Beatien Yazz, meaning "Little No Shirt." Most of his early paintings were of small

Beautiful baby girl, Ruth.

animals and birds. There was something appealing and inno-
cent or childlike in his primitive style.

Jimmy's grandmother, Little Woman, was a pretty, petite
woman whose face was very wrinkled and full of character.
Peter Bloss, a German artist visiting Wide Ruins, wanted to
paint her, so Bill helped interpret how she should sit and that
this man wanted to paint her picture. A few months after
Peter left Wide Ruins, a beautiful photograph of the oil
portrait of Little Woman arrived. The artist sent it to us as a
gift for Bill's assistance with Little Woman.

For us, this was a time of learning and growing. Our
beautiful baby girl arrived in May 1941, at the hospital in
Ganado. We figured she had universal health care. She was
delivered by a Chinese doctor who was assisted by a Mexican

nurse. My delivery room nurse was from Alaska. We were overjoyed to have a little girl, and we named her Patricia Ruth.

Sallie Lippincott was deeply involved in trying to restore the old practice of using vegetable dyes in Navajo weaving. Since he could speak the Navajo language, Bill C. helped Sallie get the Navajo women to use the vegetable dyes in their weaving. He also helped locate the plants used to make the natural dyes. I have a list that will explain what plants made certain colors. They were all beautiful, soft earth shades with no stark black or red. The bolder, darker colors were produced by aniline dyes made commercially by DuPont.

Today, the vegetal dye rugs from Wide Ruins are among the finest of Navajo rugs. There is never a border on them, and the patterns are much like the Mexican serape, a design within a stripe. The colors and designs appear delicate and blend well with any decor.

I might mention that each area where rugs are made seems to have their own distinctive colors and designs and generally use aniline dye made by DuPont. For instance, Ganado Red is produced by the type of water at Ganado plus aniline dye.

Plants for Vegetal Dyes for Wide Ruins Rugs

Material	*Color**
Walnut leaves	brown
Wild holly berries	dusty rose
Juniper berries	dull blue
Snake weed	bright yellow
Yarrow	tan
Sage	pale green
Red gila	pinkish (almost flesh tone)
Small sunflowers	caramel
Red onions	dark olive drab
Brown onion	gold
Mt. mahogany root	pinkish (deeper than red gila)
Lichens (fungus on scrub oak)	soft red
Alder bark	rust
Gray chamiso	light olive drab
Green groundsel	light yellow
Juniper mistletoe	brown
Wild blackberries	lavender (with grayish tone)
Rabbit brush	yellow
Juniper root	chocolate brown
Purple bee plant	sage
Wild walnut shells	dark brown
Canaigre dock root	camel
Gambier oak bark	light grayish brown
Prickly pear cactus	royal purple
Goldenrod	dirty yellow
Canaigre dock blossom	cocoa brown
Red cedar roots	pastel red
Wild privet root	yellow-green
Rock lichen	green-gray
Sumac leaves, piñon pitch & ocher	black

*Colors will vary in different seasons; all shades are a soft pastel.

Hosteen Nez

On the morning of October 28, 1938, I arrived at Wide Ruins about 7:00 AM. The owner, Mr. Peter Parquette, was to turn the store over to Bill Lippincott. About 8:00, the Lippincotts drove in, and we all went into the post and started inventory. It didn't take long, as Mr. Parquette had let the stock run down, so we finished around noon.

Bill Lippincott suggested that we open up, as there were a lot of Navajos outside waiting to come in. We opened the door and they started piling inside. But it wasn't like we expected. They were an unhappy group because they all had something in pawn—bracelets, beads, buckskins and such. They wanted the new owner to take over the pawn so they could redeem it at some later date. But Bill L. didn't want to take over the pawn. He considered it a losing business, because on the Reservation, you aren't allowed to charge interest and you have to keep it for years. Everyone was talking at once in loud voices.

I walked out into the bull pen and yelled to get their attention. "Quieten down and let's talk about this." I listened to the Indians' side, then turned to Bill L.: "These people are the ones you will have to trade with every day. If you want to establish good will and trust with them, I'd advise you to take their pawn."

Bill L. looked at me, then at the angry crowd. Finally, he said, "Okay, let's inventory the pawn." That decision made

Wide Ruins Trading Post, circa 1938.

everybody happy and put us both in good with the Navajos. They found that they could trust us, which is the main thing in working with them or anyone. They called me Hosteen Nez, which means "tall man."

After the purchase was final, the Lippincotts took over the Wide Ruins Trading Post in 1938, and we were in business. Jean and I lived in a large double hogan on the hill behind the post. Jean was a wonderful cook and could make a meal out of anything. She baked her own bread and, once in a while, we'd have a beef roast. Sometimes Navajo friends would bring us a leg of lamb from the reservation. We ate smoked ham that didn't have to be refrigerated and lots of canned meat.

The Lippincotts wanted to do some remodeling on their house, especially in the kitchen. When they started, it was a huge mess, and Sallie Lippincott and Mrs. Muriel Fordyce, the manager's wife, went to California for a month while carpenters were working. Bill Lippincott and the manager, J. B. Fordyce, had a hard time cooking for themselves, so Jean

Typical Navajo customers, late 1930s.

offered to cook their dinner every night. They, in turn, offered to buy the groceries.

One night they were there for dinner and Bill Lippincott said, "Let's have a drink before dinner."

"Sorry," I said. "I don't have a drop of anything here to drink."

"I do," he offered. "I'll go down to the house, and bring up a bottle."

He came back with a bottle of Vat 69 and poured us all a drink. Jean had a very small one because she didn't drink much. But we three men had a normal scotch and water. We visited for a while after dinner. Later, after they went home, I noticed that Bill L. had left his bottle of scotch. I put it up in the cabinet and forgot all about it.

A few nights later, they came up again and Lippincott said, "Let's have a drink."

I opened the cabinet. "Your bottle's still here. I keep forgetting to give it back to you."

"Fine. We'll drink that." There was still a lot of booze in that bottle, so we had our drink, then our dinner. Sitting there visiting after dinner, shooting the breeze, Bill L. said, "Let's have another drink."

Fordyce said, "Oh, no. Save it for another time. I don't want any more."

But Lippincott insisted. "I didn't get it to save. Bill Cousins will drink with me."

"Sure," I agreed. "I'll have one."

Well, when he saw us with our glasses of scotch, Fordyce gave in. "If you're going to drink it all, then I'll have one, too." So Lippincott fixed him one, and we emptied the bottle.

I was sitting on the bed talking, which was more comfortable than the nail kegs we used at the dining table. We only had a couple of comfortable chairs, and the guests had those. We sat there more than an hour visiting and drinking.

Finally, when they were ready to go, Fordyce said to Bill L. "I don't think you can walk home, Bill. Somebody might have to help you up the hill."

"Don't worry about me," Bill L. said. "I can get there all right."

They didn't say anything to me about how much I'd drunk, but I was "lit to the gills."

I just sat there quietly and said, "G'night." After they left, I could see the bed spinning around the room. When it came around again, I grabbed it and held on. Next morning, I was fine, even though I drank quite a bit that night. I never had a hangover from scotch whiskey in my life.

After we had been at Wide Ruins about seven months, Bill Lippincott came to me and said, "We'd like you to stay on permanently with us. I'll raise your wages."

"I was thinking about going to California," I answered.

Behind the counter at Wide Ruins Trading Post, left to right: Bill Cousins, Bill Lippincott, and J. B. Fordyce with Navajo customers.

"Well, if that's what your heart's set on, I can't stop you. But I'll give you more money if you'll stay. And you won't have to live in that old hogan anymore. I'll build you a modern house on the hill with a bathtub, shower, everything—the works."

It sure sounded good. "I'll stay." I continued to work at Wide Ruins for Bill Lippincott until the war, and he sold the post to Carl Hine. J. B. Fordyce left Wide Ruins after working there about a year.

Soon after we started trading in 1938, Sallie and Bill Lippincott wanted to get the old-style vegetal dye rugs started again. I was instructed to talk to the Navajo women who did the weaving. "Tell them you won't refuse to buy their aniline rugs, but offer them such a low price, they'll take them elsewhere." Sure enough, Sallie was right. The Navajo women would take their rugs away to another post to sell. But

Dan Gaddy and Joe Toddy behind the counter at Wide Ruins, late 1930s.

before they left, I would say, "If this were a vegetal dye rug, we would have given you a real good price for it, more than the aniline dye rug."

After about eight months of losing their business, a Navajo woman named Louise Dale came into the post with a small vegetal dye rug. We paid almost double what we would have paid for an aniline dye rug, then hung it on the wall in the trading post. As the weavers came in, we would show them the rug and tell them how much we paid for it. From then on, the weavers in the area began trying to make vegetal dye rugs. They experimented on their own to discover what wild plants and roots would give certain colors and different shades. They even used lichen off the oak trees, onion skins, rabbit weed, red cedar roots and juniper berries to come up with some very pleasing colors for their rugs.

We bought vegetal dye rugs almost exclusively because the other traders in the area thought they were ugly and unsalable. In about five or six years, though, they saw what we were doing, and we began to get competition for these rugs. The trader at Burnt Water, Stanley Smith, was our strongest competition. The vegetal dye rugs were unique and beautiful, and by the time the post sold in 1950, there was a great demand for vegetal dye rugs.

Several Navajos lived near the post and worked there occasionally. Hosteen Glish stocked the shelves, and Paul Jones worked with the horses and did yard maintenance. Dan Gaddy was a good plumber, and his younger brother, Roy, was drafted in the war and was sent to the South Pacific and wrote letters back to us to keep us posted on his travels. Another man who worked with us was Joe Toddy. He was a good handyman and generally took care of the Lippincotts house when they went away. Joe's young son, Jimmy, was a very good artist and was always drawing pictures on any old thing he could find. Bill L. and Sallie took him under their wing and fixed him a desk in one of the warerooms, gave him his first crayolas and later watercolors and oil paints.

One summer, Peter Bloss, an artist from Germany, came to visit and paint or draw some of the Indians in the area. Peter didn't believe in wearing much clothing, just a pair of old Levis with the legs cut off, a pair of sandals, and a big sombrero. He preferred to go without a shirt. When he came around, the Indians made jokes about him, in the Navajo language, of course. I was always joking around with our customers, so I said, "You shouldn't tease this poor man. He's so hard up, he has no shirt." After that, the Indians called him No Shirt.

One day little Jimmy Toddy came running through the post in a hurry to get to his painting in the wareroom. He wasn't wearing a shirt. I just commented, "There goes Little No Shirt." And the name stuck. He liked it and began signing his paintings Beatien Yazz, meaning "Little No Shirt."

Bill L. and Sallie did a lot for the Navajos of our community. They built a leather tanning shop for them. Then they stocked it with all the chemicals needed to tan hides into leather, all at no charge.

The Navajos were highly superstitious of lightning, coyotes, bears, death, snakes, and a house where someone had died. They wouldn't kill a snake. At Wide Ruins, there were lots of rattlesnakes, and I was concerned about the kids' safety. The Navajos who lived around there told me there was a big den of snakes nearby, with hundreds of snakes that hibernate there every fall. In the spring, they come out.

I wanted to know where they were: "Show me where they are."

"No, you'll kill them," they always told me.

"That's right. You bet I will."

One year, about the last of September or early October when the weather was getting chilly, a Navajo named Big Shorty, who lived close to the snakepit, came to the post saying, "A snake nearly bit me. He came into my hogan, came after me. Sure was mad! Come on, and I'll show you where that snake bin is."

I'd been there several years and nobody had told me where those snakes were. "If I go," I told him, "I'll take my shotgun and kill some snakes."

He agreed. "That's why I want you to go."

So I took my twelve-gauge shotgun and killed many rattle-snakes that day. Must have been about fifty. Every fall after that, I'd go down there and kill some snakes. Just before I left for California, I bought some dynamite and stuffed a stick in each of the seven big holes under the rocks where they hibernated. I set it off and blew up that entire den of rattlesnakes. As far as I know, there were never any more snakes around the trading post.

One time when Edward was about five or six, he went to visit his teacher, who lived across the road from the post. Sylvia Sample was a stout, strong young woman who practiced wrestling with her mother until she broke her mother's finger and her dad made her stop the wrestling. While Edward was there, we had a heavy rain, so I started to go after him. The wash which separated us was suddenly filled with a flash flood. Sylvia and Edward stood on the other side with the water running high and fast.

"I'll throw him across, and you catch him," she said. Poor Edward wanted none of that. I figured she could probably toss him, but how far? About that time, a Navajo came along on horseback and carried Edward back to me. He was much happier with that solution.

On the night of May 4, 1941, with spring rains and muddy roads, I drove Jean from Wide Ruins to the Sage Memorial Hospital in Ganado. The staff took Jean right in and told me it would be a while before our new baby came. They put me in a room where I could stay until time. About 2:30 in the morning, someone came with the good news that our daughter had been born. Mother and baby were fine, and we decided to name her Patricia Ruth. I returned to Wide Ruins a happy new father.

Soon after World War II started, around 1942, we had to take an inventory of all the merchandise at Wide Ruins that was to be rationed. That included sugar, coffee, all canned meats, shoes, and tires. It kind of took me by surprise when I found out that I couldn't buy any more than what I actually had on hand right then.

You could order only as much as you had stamps for, even if it was just one ten-pound bag at a time, which would not have been enough for our stock. The inventory was real low on sugar and coffee, probably because it was almost time to reorder when rationing went into effect. I was honest about it and tried to get more of an allotment, so we could keep a bigger stock on hand, at least a week's supply of coffee and sugar. But the Office of Price Administration, the federal bureau that issued rationing stamps, wouldn't allow me any more. The OPA also controlled and regulated prices, which was all right, for our prices were low anyway.

Meantime, somebody stole twelve three-pound cans of coffee from the post's storage, and that cut our supply even shorter. I couldn't figure what happened to that coffee. Finally, Hosteen Glish, one of the Navajo men who worked at the post, told me that Joe Toddy, who also worked there and was the father of Little No Shirt, took it. Well, I jumped him about it, and Joe admitted taking it. He said his family and friends were short on coffee. I held a little money out of his wages from time to time for it, but there wasn't much I could do about it. Losing that coffee really put me in short supply. I tried again getting coffee and sugar from the OPA without success, because the amount you could order was based on the inventory figure that was taken at the beginning of rationing.

You took your stamps for sugar, coffee, meat, and any other products you needed to the bank in Gallup where you had an account and did business. Each item had its own account, which you wrote checks on for the amount of whatever item you were ordering. Finally, we got smart about using the rationing stamps and found a way to increase the post's inventory. I went to our bank and took ten ten-pound stamps for one hundred pounds of sugar. When I filled out the deposit slip, I just added the extra zero to make it read one thousand pounds. I figured that if the bank said anything about it, I would tell them that I had added that extra zero by mistake. But when I handed over the stamps, the bank teller never even counted them, just threw them into an envelope, put the deposit slip on file, and threw the envelope with the stamps in the trash. He gave me the credit I needed for a thouand pounds of sugar, and I had enough sugar in my inventory to last a month or so.

Later, I did the same thing for coffee, but we didn't have to do that with any other product. We didn't sell much fresh meat, only some canned meats like corned beef, Vienna sausage, Spam, and sardines. We occasionally got some pickled pigs' feet, which I enjoyed with beer, but the Navajos wouldn't touch them. Thought they were dirty. The Navajos didn't buy much meat from us because they had their own beef and sheep. The OPA figured we could get fresh meat from the packing houses.

The Navajos would come into the post with their ration books, maybe eight or ten of them, and they'd want only two or three cans of tomatoes, coffee, flour, lard, or whatever. The rest of their stamps were wasted. So we'd take all the stamps in the book and let the Navajos buy whatever they wanted, since they always had more stamps than they needed. We used the excess stamps for supplies, especially coffee, sugar, and canned goods.

We had many excess meat stamps and soon learned that some of the people in Gallup didn't have enough meat for their families. I took my excess meat stamps to the butcher shop in Gallup and gave them to Chano Gonzales, the butcher, and told him to just give credit to anyone who needed meat and was short of stamps. Bob did the same thing at Cousins Brothers Trading Post.

I never had enough gasoline or tires during the rationing. I started with an A card, which allowed fifteen gallons of gas per month, and that had to be posted on your car windshield. I went to the Ration Board in Chambers, Arizona, and talked to Mr. Root, the head man. He also sold insurance policies for New York Life Insurance Company. I said, "I really need more gas. I work at Wide Ruins, and it's so far out of town. And while you're at it, I need to buy a life insurance policy."

"Yes," he said. "I can see you need more gas living so far out. You should have a B card." The B card entitled the owner to a little more gas, and that kept me going for a while.

Finally, after a few more trips and a few more policies, he ended up giving me the highest gas card allotment, the C card. My brother, Bob, couldn't get such a high gas card, so I told him, "Bring your pickup loaded with a fifty-five-gallon barrel, and I can let you have some gasoline." Which he did.

If I needed tires, I'd go to Mr. Root and say, "I really need tires. And while we're at it, I'll need another life insurance policy."

He'd say, "Well, you're helping the war effort, and I can see you need tires." So he'd give me the okay for four tires. I ended up with seven of those dang policies, worth about a thousand each.

On the post, our refrigerator ran on propane, but I had to buy a white, leadfree gas for the Kohler Light Plant, a small gasoline generator which supplied electricity for our lights and water pump. We were given enough gas to run it twenty-four hours a day, but we only ran it six hours at night, so we didn't use it all up. They were supposed to put a package of dye in that white gasoline that went into the Kohler, so the government could make sure you used that gas just for the electricity. But I talked them out of putting the dye in, saying it didn't look good. Then I'd sell Bob the gasoline, and that way we both had enough to get by on.

When World War II started, Bill Lippincott joined the navy as a lieutenant commander. Home on leave, he came to see me at Wide Ruins and asked, "Bill, do you think you'll be called to service?"

"Yes, probably will. That's why I'm moving to California, so Jean can be near her mother if I have to go."

"Well, I'm going to sell the place to Carl Hine. He's offered to buy it, and I plan to buy it back from him after the war is over. If you would stay until at least until November 1 and collect all accounts for me, I'd appreciate it."

So, for Bill Lippincott, I agreed to stay. I didn't care for Carl Hine at the time, but after I got to know him, I liked him very much. Many years later, he turned out to be a good friend. But there was one thing about him that stuck in my craw, and I couldn't forget it.

When we were trying to make it at God's Little Acre and Smith opened a post near us at Pine Haven, it cut off my trade. I went everywhere looking for a job, even tried to get a job mining coal. But there were no jobs to be had anywhere. I went to Gross Kelly, a wholesale grocery, hardware, and dry goods store that also bought wool, rugs, and jewelry from traders, and spoke to the manager, Carl Hine. I asked him for a job saying, "I'll do most anything if you'll give me a chance."

He laughed like the dickens and said, "Hell, no, if there was any work around here to do, I'd do it myself." Everybody in the office heard him and laughed, too. They all thought it was a funny joke. But I didn't think it was funny, and I remembered it.

In July 1942, Carl Hine took over the Wide Ruins post. As I promised Bill Lippincott, I continued to work for him until November, when I collected all the accounts from the Indians who owed the post. The Navajos didn't like to pay a debt to someone else. They figured they owed me, not another fellow. If I wasn't there to collect, they might not pay. So I collected all the accounts, then told Carl I planned to leave for California. He wanted me to stay on and work for him, but I refused.

"Why? I can't understand why you won't just stay on. I'll give you a salary plus 40 percent profit."

But I stood my ground. "You'll understand when I tell you this story." I told him about the time I was desperate for a job and went to him at Gross Kelly, how he laughed at me and said "Hell, no."

"Carl, I'll never forget that. I had to tuck my tail between my legs and go back home, and I couldn't support my family. It was hard, and I won't work for you now."

Carl apologized and said, "Bill, if I'd only known you, you could have had any job you wanted. I wish I'd helped you, and I realize how hard it must have been. I'd like to make it up to you, if you'll stay on."

I shook my head stubbornly. "It's too late." So I turned down more money than I'd ever made and, after the lambs were shipped, we took off for California.

California

Eager to seek a new lifestyle in California, Jean and Bill moved their family with high hopes. For years, they had heard about California and thought about living there several times. However, when the promised good life was not fulfilled, their reasons for loving the Southwest became evident. After living for only a few months in the golden state, leaving became inevitable.

Notice that their recollections of exactly why they went to California differ. At that point, Jean was involved almost exclusively with her young family, while Bill was thrust into scrambling for jobs during World War II. His experiences reveal the state of the country at that time and his own disillusionment with graft and corruption. It is interesting to compare the elaborate negotiations for the first position at Wide Ruins with the Lippincotts and this one, where Bill wired, "You name the terms." A relationship of trust had been established on both sides.

Despite their differing views about California living, Jean and Bill agreed wholeheartedly on the return to their beloved open skies and far horizons of the Southwest—and soon! After years of living in the beauty of the outdoors, the sunny weather, and the camaraderie and independence of post life, it's no wonder that they hated their confining jobs and crowded lifestyle in California.

Up to Our Ears

Hitler's army was on the move in Europe, and this disrupted all our lives. Bill Lippincott, being in the naval reserves, began making preparations to go. He and Sallie had decided to lease or sell the post to friends with an option to buy back. In October 1943 we began making plans to move ourselves to California. Bill C. made crates, and we packed. It was hard to leave loved ones in the Gallup area, but things looked good in California. My parents had retired there, so they sort of showed us the way around.

In California, Bill found work at a bomb factory in Azusa, near Pasadena. After a few months he was not feeling too well from breathing the gases and decided to look for other work. The company, American Cyanide and Chemical, threatened to have him drafted if he left. Bill said that would be fine with him. He had tried to enlist, but the service had turned him down because he had a family and was needed at home.

He got another job and things were going well, but by then, we had California up to our ears. What a dreary place. We missed the wide open spaces, lots of beautiful sunshine, and starlit nights of the Southwest. We had been eight months in California, enough for a very long time. Then one day a telegram arrived from Bill Lippincott asking if we would consider going back to Wide Ruins to run the post for him. Oh happy day!

Bill almost ran to the telegraph office across the street to send the message: "I'm on the way. We will work out details later."

Palms to Grease

Jean's folks, Cordie and Dick, went to California, where they had financed a cafe for Jean's Aunt Alice. By the time they got there, Alice took off, leaving them stuck with the business. So we went to California to help Cordie and to find work. I got a job as a carpenter with a contractor working for Douglas Aircraft in El Segundo, California, building what was supposed to be the largest aircraft hangar in the world. We rented a house from an old friend who also went out there to seek his fortune, Howard Wirtz from Cousins Brothers days. Three of us car pooled from Baldwin Park to El Segundo, about fifty miles round trip daily. We used a different fellow's car each week.

Many days it rained us out, and we couldn't work all day. I had a family with two children by then and needed the money from a full day's work. Well, the rain continued pouring and, since we worked outside, we had to quit early most every day. Finally we decided that we couldn't make a living that way, so Howard Wirtz and I started building or remodeling small homes on our own time.

Lumber was rationed, so we'd have to go from one lumber yard to another to buy enough wood to do a job. We were doing all right, making more money than when we were working for wages. I decided I'd better build myself a house, so in between jobs or on Sundays and at night, I'd work on my house.

After I got it built, some people from the OPA came to the house, and they were very unhappy with me. They said that it was unlawful for me to build a house during this time of rationing and war. After arguing for about fifteen minutes, I told them, "The house is built. And I did it. No use beating around the bush about it. It's done. I admit to doing it. Now, you do your thing. If you have a case against me, arrest me and take me to jail."

My father-in-law, Dick Dunaway, spoke up for me. "What's the matter with you fellows? You know a man has to have a place to live. What's wrong in that?" The OPA officials couldn't argue that and finally left. I didn't hear any more from them. There was really nothing they could do. Now, I think they wanted a little pay under the table to leave me alone. But they didn't get it from me.

I had a similar problem with gasoline. After we'd been working in California a while, one of Howard's kids got into serious trouble with the law. The judge told Howard to take his sixteen-year-old son out of the state, and they'd drop the charges. So, Howard and his family left. I couldn't do all that work alone, because it was really a two-man job, so I went to work for American Cyanamid Chemical Company in Azusa, California. There, I loaded cyanide gas into five-hundred- or thousand-pound bombs. These bombs were made of heavy cast iron and stood about four and a half feet high. They'd roll the bombs into the bomb booth where I sat, and I'd fill them through a hole in the wall. The gas liquefied at seventeen or eighteen degrees below zero. When I filled it, I had to put the cap or plug on the top.

Driving back and forth from Bassett, California, where the house was built, to Azusa for this job six days a week took more gas than I was allowed. I went to the OPA in El Monte, California, and told them my problem. I drove to work with three passengers whose wives had to use their cars to go to work, and I needed more gasoline. The OPA said it was impossible to get more gas and I'd have to do something else.

"Okay," I said. "I'll find a way." I walked out of the building.

One of those guys I had talked to came out and said, "Hey, I can get you that gasoline you need. A ten-dollar bill will get it for you."

I was furious. "No. The men who run the black market are pretty low life, but they're more American than you. I have no use for the OPA. I'll just buy my gas on the black market." And that's what I did.

I felt that I was doing my part for the war effort because I was making bombs for the war. That group at the OPA just wanted their palms greased, and I wouldn't do it.

One evening I returned home from work and found a letter from Bill Lippincott. He wondered if I would be interested in taking over the Wide Ruins Trading Post for him, as Mr. Hine had decided to sell. Bill L. had first option to repurchase the post. He asked on what terms I would come back to Wide Ruins. There was a Western Union close by our house, and I walked (maybe ran) right over there and sent him a wire. "I am on my way to Wide Ruins. You name the terms." Was I ever glad to leave California.

Wide Ruins: Tales and Times

Beneath the current Navajo community of Wide Ruins and the crumbling traces of the Wide Ruins Post lie the scattered and buried remnants of an ancient village called Kin Teel, meaning "wide" (or "broad") "house." Archaeologic surveys record that a large prehistoric village site, including a kiva and, at one time, a two-story adobe house, remain hidden in the small hills peppered with vermillion pebbles and lava gravel. The Navajos and old-time traders have always known of those ruins. Local resident Crip Chee valued the turquoise beads that he found around the property as a special gift from the Diné (pronounced "din-ay"), his ancestors.

The Navajo soldiers' letters reveal much about the impact of worldly experience in contrast to their naive and peaceful existence on the reservation. We see the difficulty of Navajo families dealing with sons and husbands who were sent to the war front, as well as the loneliness of the young Navajo men who were forced abruptly into another culture, to fight a war about which they knew little. With the end of World War II, jobs and relationships between the trader and the Navajo began to change.

At age forty, Bill faced another career move, and we are reminded of present-day down-sizing and forced early retirement. Again, he took charge and singlehandedly purchased a house for the family, assuming Jean would like it. And, of course, she did. Meantime, Jean had the knowledge and skills to temporarily take over Bill's job at Wide Ruins, although she still was not paid for her work. But her role was changing.

Back to Heaven on Earth

The man who bought Wide Ruins from Bill Lippincott was in poor health and was only too glad for Bill to repurchase the post. And we were only too glad to be living back there.

The Navajo men were not only going to war but off the reservation to work in other places, mainly for the railroad. Bill C. was appointed by the Railroad Retirement Board to sign up workers from our area, thus creating a pool of available workers. They recruited from this list for a long time, and it certainly broadened the Navajo work world.

The men worked in Chicago, Washington, Oregon, Idaho, Wyoming, Utah, California, Colorado, and Texas. When they came home from a job after being laid off, they were immediately eligible to sign up again. For the most part, they were good to send their wages home to their families. Quite often they brought back nice gifts.

During this time, in addition to helping at the post and taking care of our family, I was, as most traders' wives were, the correspondent for the workers as well as for the service boys. They sent their allotments and war bonds to their families through me. I still have some of the letters, especially from Dan and Roy Gaddy, who worked at the store for us:

Left to right: Jean and Bill Cousins and Bill and Sallie Lippincott behind the counter at Wide Ruins Trading Post with Navajo customers, circa 1945.

Ft. Wingate New Mexico
March 20, 1943

Hi Bill C.

Last week we left Kinteel. We stay at Chambers all afternoon. The buss didn't stop for us. Just when by we flag then down. The buss drive he just point his two fingers at us we don't know what the "hell" that mean.

Until six o'lock. The Sante Fe Buss pick us up and we roll a long to old Gallup N. Mex and Hush-Be-toh School. We stop at the Gallup for thirty minutes then we when on to Wingate. We walk in three miles on highway to school. We reach our distination about 10 o'lock in nite. Tom Lee he got sick that nite and miss a day on his work. He's ok, now. he singing Navajo squaw dance song.

Bill, please give my wife whatever she needs. I pay my bill in near future. don't worry.

Sincerely yours,

Dan Gaddy

— —

Bitter Creek Wyo.
c/o Glenn Varley s Store
Sept. 3. 1943

Dear Bill C.

"Hi Bill." How you doing now. I hope your still smile like you use to Bill.

I hope your always that way. When you left the Kin-teel Trdg post. I hope you will remember us people around Kinteel trdg pt. If you do. Write us a letters. deep in the heart of Kinteel's. "This going to be long time no see." or many moon. Heap big Chief all work on the railroad road.

All the boys from Wide Ruins are doing fine so do I. This is the second day since we arrive here. at Bitter Creek Wyo. It's about the same as Arizona and the weather is the same.

The only well known people are working here is color people no others. And Indians. Navajo twentyeight of us. they ship us here.

I wrote to my wife and tell her that I wish she could send my ration book to me. Just as soon as possible. See that dose that too. They wanted us our ration book. To buy food stuff. Will them. I need very badly.

Yours truly

Dan Gaddy

— —

Grants, New Mexico
c/o R.R. Depot
Oct. 5, 1944

Dear B. Cousin

I'm over here at the Grants N. Mex. With Two boys from Kinteel. We are doing fine over here. The weather is kind cold in the morning. But rest of day warm. Only the mountain Grants had a sheet of snow one morning that's was last week.

Beside three of us their three more guys from Klage-toh. We know their very well and Peter Lee left us here Oct 2. he said he was gone home. and to induction.

I like to know how I stand with my account Bill at you store. Bill C. also I like to know where I stop the last on my accounts went I got five dollar. Bill from you that day. Did she got some more stuff from you lately How much did she trade out, reason I said this is she was trade on my account for somebody else and charge it to me. I just hear this not very long ago. If she going to continuation trading for some else again she sure will be sorry. You tell this to her. If she wanted to terminable that's alright with me. And if she wanted to continue with it that is up to her. If she gots to use herself not someone. Or she had a reason for it to? etc

P.S. Tell her send my leather coat and rain coat & gray blanket, luncheon bucket.

If she doesn't wanted to send this to me in two day went receive this message. Tell my father he'll get the keys for hogan. Let him bring this stuff up to you, and you will send this to me. All in one package. Please B. Cousin I depend on you. Just charge the postage to me on my account book. When you are send this drop me letter or cards. Best regard to you.

Yours truley

Dan Gaddy.

Send Roy Gaddy address to me.

Dan's younger brother, Roy Gaddy, was awfully lonesome after he was drafted and wrote us from his posts in the Pacific:

17th Batt
c/o F.P.O. San Francis Calif
March 30, 1945

Dear Mr Cousins,
Certainly glad to get a whole of your correspondent again also at anytime. I am just as happy as little bee when I hear from you and tell me everything from home.
You sure put mine thought in side out. I alway forget to say hello to each one of the mans are in the store daily. Also too your folks.
Well I will say keep the bonds like it is, and other money I send you keep it in cash. Very glad my mother want to save some for me too. Very gladly to here that. I'm feel much better about it.
Of course I have many brothers beside me. Let them help there mother and daddy for change. so they don't get along in hard way of there parents. Maybe they think I will take care as long as they live.
It very nice where I staying. Very nice lands too. I like it here as well as kinteel, and many boys they do like it too, as well as I do!
I will sign off here. Say a big hello to Mr and Mrs Cousins. Good nite.
Always wish you luck
Wrtie me again some time

Lee Roy G. sl/c

———

c/o Fleet post office
San Francisco, Calif.
July 25, 1945

Dear Mr & Mrs Cousins,
The letter you send me reach me again.
I being busy so I did answer it back over a week. Anyway I dont say much. I'm very glad to tell me about that bonds. I don't no what they look like it too. I never see our buy one

yet. Since I being in new place there is a lot hard works so it keep us very busy. I hate so much every thing. Rains & mud and it get so hot and dry up and that dust really bad too. I got too much trouble with every thing. Could hardly what I like to do. The only time I feel better is when I get letter from some one think of me. Letter take a long time to reach me Some time I dont have any mail. I think to myself maybe my home folks forgot about me.

They think war is over I guess. Anyway it very hard for them to tell me what they think. They just thinkin I am beyond sea somewhere and they don't no what it really look like out here and what kind of a people's liveing beyond the seas. I never did see any Navajo boys when I came here in a new place. just wish to see one, But I never did go around much just working around our camp. A lot of work to do,

I just think about our farm how it came out this year. Maybe no one think much about it. All they look at is that moneys they received from me So I think it does not do them any good. They spend too much of it, also I don't think those brother's never send any money too there daddy & mother. Poor man like me try to do everything I can. But the brothers don't care for anything. I work day after day and week after week. Now I being so tired don't no where to think. Close here and many good wish.

Sincerely yours,

Roy Gaddy

— —

c/o F.P.O. San Francis. Calif.
16th of Aug. 1945

Dear Mrs. Cousins

I will write you again tonite, well I am very safe now and nothing much to worried about, I'm happy to hear the war is over in pacific now.

All I waiting for is mine transportation to take me back too the states.

I haveing hear anything yet what they going doing with some us fellow. I know very well about oldes mens. They will get out soon first.

I don't no about myself. How long I'll stay in when I return to state's.

They probable keep me for a while, I hope not, I think I'll enroll for school again. Any kind of transing.

I really get drunk when I hear the war is over, and next day I was so damn sick I feel like new man There is not much news in me. We're all glad too here war is over and they really did shouting at night just like 4th of July Ganging away at midnight. Some boys it shoot. They really did no there they shooting at they're so excited about war is over.

They are really when happy bee. Maybe you hear about it and all over the states now, I would like to aks you. Send my grandmama name to me next time when you write me again.

I'll drop her a line as soon as I get her name. I don't no how she spell her name, Hello's too each one of you back home's. I met one Navay girl here on Pyukyus Islands. Her home is at Ganado Ariz. It very nice to meet her out here, I talk to her for long while. Well I will close here tonight.

Good nite & good day.

Sincerely yours Roy Gaddy

— —

17th Batt.
c/o F.P.O. San Francisco, Calif.
10th of Sept 1945

Dear Mrs. Cousins,

Tonite I am taking my time to answer your delightful letter which reach me again. First I'll thank you very much for everything you have done for me. Yes I am on okinawa. I am okinawa native now.

The island is big but not as good as saipan. Some mens from 17th Batt get there order to have discharge. I saw several indians boys too, I just see them around when I go for a ride around the island. Naha is really smash in they bomb the hell of that city and several Japanese City on okinawa.

Well glad to past on the news to me How the thing are around kinteel. Like to here from anyone. Some time if I dont have any mail It seem I don't have any folks are friend It hurt my feeling a lot. Some time I wish mine brothers or sister write me with out receive any letter from me But they never do it. One of Wingate teachers write me very often and alway send me package. just like one of her own son. But my own parent never do think of me much

Dont no what they had me for just put me in hard life. Good nite ans. soon again.

from R. Gaddy

— —

17th N.C. Batt. Co #3
F.P.O. San Francis. Calif.
Oct. 7, 1945

Dear Mr Willie,

Today is Sunday I have takeing end enasy. We don't work seven days a week anymore. There is no place to go and nothing much to do around camp. I have enought going around the island and no other place I can go. That I never had been on this island of Okinawa.

So I might as well stay home and get more rest for next week. There is very few mens left in 17th Batt. with me. All the boys I have know they all when back to U.S. for discharge.

So I am not feel ing so good about I don't know anybody to be friend. I really dont have a good news that I can mention to you Bill. All I know is I will be here next year. It hard to say when I will be in U.S. and home Well I have a hard time nothing is good to me on this island of Japanese territory. They can give it back to Japanese one again. That all I can say aobut htis island of Okinawa.

P.S. Well Willie I order for some picture to California. And I said they will send it to you at Wide Ruins. If the photos come to you. Sell it to the peoples Maybe they like to have one or two set of it. They are all different kind of photos. Action of saipan and here okinawa and other place in pacific area.

I dont no when they will send it to you. if it come, sell it out for me. Made $250 a set? All to-gether are 13, set of photos. If they buy some safe the money for me.

That all I can tell you now and thank very much Bill.

Oh yeah Mr. Willie They give me another rate, CM3/c.

I was very glad to get it and the crow. Hope that crow will never fly off from my arms and keep it and let Mom and daddy will see it. I'll try to be god to myself. Good by Mr Willie and Mr Jean.

Sincerely,
From Roy Gaddy CM3/c

Patrick was another young man who lived at Wide Ruins:

Alooha
August 21, 1943

Dear Bill,

Received your letter this morning. Was very glad to hear from you again Bill. This letter been written on 3rd of August. Just got it today. When are you leaving Bill? Try write to me, when you get on your job, will you Bill.

I haven't much to say. I should go to town, this evening. But I'm so lazy to go place. I'm doing pretty good all this time. The weather is pretty fair, out here. How is out that way? Around here, most of the time, it rainning.

Today it pretty fine day. But it look like it gonno rain again. I don't think they have any rain in Arizona. Boy this is pretty place, in summer, I don't know on winter time. I think its cold. Well Bill I better close here. I'll write again soon as I can. Wishe you good luck Bill.

Very Sincerely Yours,

Pfc. Patrick Footracer

One summer, a friend of Sallie Lippincott from back East, Alberta Hannum, visited Wide Ruins. She poked around, meeting and talking to everyone. We didn't know what she was doing, other than being a pest. Pretty soon we found out she was writing a book about the Lippincotts and Jimmy Toddy, Beatien Yazz. She called it *Spin a Silver Dollar* and got the title idea from my husband, Bill, who would spin a silver dollar on the store counter to intrigue and entertain the Indians. They were fascinated by the motion of that coin; it seemed to charm them.

The book must have been a bestseller, for people would drive the sixteen miles off Highway 66 and come into the post at Wide Ruins and say, "I've read the book. Where are the Lippincotts? We'd like to meet them."

The Lippincotts often traveled and were not at the post much of the time. So usually I would answer, "I don't know. I don't keep up with them." The visitors were always disappointed, as they were only interested in meeting the Lippincotts. Several years later Alberta wrote another book about Jimmy and his art called *Paint the Wind.*

Once Ansel Adams was out at Wide Ruins taking pictures. He needed a black focusing cloth to cover his camera that he had set up on a tripod. I was so green that I didn't realize he was a famous photographer. But I was willing to help: "I'll be happy to fix you one, if you'll tell me what you need."

"I'll pay you for it," he offered.

It was such a simple request that I couldn't imagine taking money for it. "No charge. Nothing to it." So I fixed him a cover out of some black cloth we had at the store.

Some weeks after that, a large envelope came in the mail to me. Inside was a beautiful 8" x 10" photograph of Ruth, who was about four years old, taken in courtyard of the Wide Ruins Post. I value that photo, which I now know was taken by a master photographer and a very nice man.

Photo taken of Ruth by Ansel Adams after Jean made a black cloth for him, 1946.

Another visitor to Wide Ruins was John Adair, an expert on Indian silversmithing, who wrote an excellent book, *The Navajo and Pueblo Silversmiths.* He and his wife stayed for some time in the guest house, and they had a cat named Nes-Bah. Often at dusk we could hear them calling, "Nes-Bah! Nes-Bah!" I always thought that was a funny name for a cat. Nes-Bah is a popular female Navajo name.

We found that the Navajos were unmerciful at making fun of each other. Crip Chee, so named because of a deformed hand, was one colorful character who lived at Wide Ruins and provided plenty of laughs. Crip Chee was a gambler and fine moccasin maker. He had been commissioned by one of the Lippincotts' friends to make a pair of moccasins. He finished one shoe but kept putting off making the mate. There were so many interesting things to do, like gambling games, sings and ceremonials, and such. While he was away from home, his poor wife was often out of food. Of course, we made sure that she did not starve.

It so happened that Crip had a highly prized and most unique string of turquoise beads with several small fetish carvings that had been gleaned from Kin Teel, meaning "wide house," the ancient dwellings which lay beneath the Wide Ruins Post and grounds. I think most of the beads in this special necklace came from the earth where rains and erosion uncovered them, so Crip felt they were very special. After heavy rains, we would often visit the red ant hills and look for tiny turquoise or shell (wampum) beads, already drilled, that the ants brought out from their nests.

During one of Crip Chee's long absences, Mrs. Chee, in need of money, pawned his precious fetish and turquoise beads. These beads were brought out only in dire emergencies and never for very much money and they usually were redeemed as quickly as possible. About this time, one of the Chee's sons died of TB. We loaned him funeral clothing, including a quilt and Pendleton robe. Crip promised to pay us back, but this debt was not resolved, either. So he had accumulated quite a healthy deficit.

Finally, a good time later, Crip wanted to go to Non-Joshie (Gallup) and offered Bill C. the handsome sum of two dollars for a ride. Bill said, "I hadn't planned a trip to town and don't know when I'll be going, but I'll take the two dollars to pay on your bill."

Crip said, "I might pay a few dollars on that bill if you'll take me to Non-Joshie."

Bill answered, "Well, you don't owe much anymore."

Crip stopped short in his tracks and grinned with a gleam in his eyes. "Oh yes, I forgot. I paid you, didn't I?"

"No," Bill answered. "You didn't pay. But your wife brought your beads to pawn a few days ago, and I just took them against your bill. So you don't have to worry about paying me any more." Crip was furious with her for pawning his beloved beads. But it was not too long before he got to work, paid the bill, and retrieved his beads.

Eventually Crip finished the commissioned moccasins. Only trouble was, he made the mistake of creating both shoes for the same foot. I don't know if his Navajo buddies ever let him live that one down.

On occasion, the missionaries would send barrels of clothing for the Indians. One cold, winter day, Crip rode on horseback over the hill to the post wearing a nice, warm bathrobe that he had been given from the missionary barrel. The trading post bull pen was full that day, so Crip's arrival made quite a scene. He thought that was the greatest coat he had ever had and paraded around quite proudly. That brought forth a loud guffaw from all gathered there. The Navajos made fun of him like nobody's business. "Look at Crip. He don't know a bathrobe from a coat. That's what the white man takes a bath in!" That old man was so mad he was about to burst, and he stomped out and rode home at a hard gallup. He didn't return for a long time, until his wounded pride had healed somewhat. And he never wore that bath-robe again.

Another interesting character was a fellow named Joe Mar-tin. His wife, Big Fat Patsy, was Crip Chee's daughter and a wonderful weaver. They had a herd of sheep that made old-time, long-staple wool. These longer strands of wool pro-duced a better quality rug.

Joe had odd tastes in food. Each day for lunch, he came to the post and asked for a bottle of "catcher" (catsup). He mixed it with water and made cold tomato soup. Then his tastes took an odd turn and he started buying rubbing alcohol. Bill C. suspected what he was doing and told him he was absolutely *not* to drink it, because it was dangerous stuff. But Joe had his problem solved and told Bill he mixed it with water and sugar and it was "pretty good, alright."

Sad to say, it didn't take long to bring about his demise. His wife, Big Fat Patsy, didn't grieve long. Soon she produced twins, a no-no among the Diné (Navajo people). They seemed to think twins came from two fathers. The doctors at Ganado's Sage Memorial Hospital struggled to keep the tiny twins alive, but both finally gave up the fight and went on to a happier place.

Patsy continued her lifestyle and finally used up all that prize herd of long-staple wool sheep. Eventually the herd was completely gone and Patsy wasn't far behind.

A side note: When our daughter was born, we named her Patricia Ruth, thinking we had given her the name of no one we knew. Then we were reminded that we knew Old Fat Patsy. We quickly started calling her Ruth, after the biblical Ruth, which my mother thought was a most beautiful name. We certainly did not want to call her Patsy.

The two Bills (Cousins and Lippincott) were able to locate another source of the old-time, long-staple wool sheep and bought a small herd of the sheep for a Navajo man who lived at the Wide Ruins community named Hosteen Klitsoi, meaning "yellow man." The provision was that he would sell all the wool back to the post, which he did.

One day at the post, Bill C. was wearing a pair of trousers that were too short for his long legs. When he stepped out from behind the counter, a young Navajo woman noticed his short pants. "Billy Cousins," she said, "why don't you pull up your shoes?" Everyone had a good laugh at Bill's expense. That young woman was Annie Wauneka, daughter of Chee Dodge, the first tribal chairman of the Navajo nation. Annie later served many years on the Navajo tribal council.

One of the most exciting things to happen while were at Wide Ruins was the murder. It seems there was a triangle of unrequited love imagined by a Navajo named Ned Striker who was un poco loco. He decided he wanted another man's wife. Charlie Mike, his wife, two young daughters, and old grandmother lived not too far from the post. Neither the husband nor the wife were agreeable to Ned's strange desires.

One night, Ned went to the Mike house and attacked Charlie, his wife, and their young daughter. The oldest daughter had gone to herd sheep with the grandmother, who lived nearby, but not with the family. When the grandmother and oldest daughter returned that evening, they found the family's hogan door was locked, and it was never left that way. They could hear a child crying inside. They went for help and finally got the door open. There they found Charlie and his wife beaten to death with a tire iron. The child's skull had been crushed, and her eye was hanging out. She died about a month later.

Word spread fast to the store. The two Bills went to see what had happened. The FBI was called, for it was a crime on federal land, and they started questioning the Navajos. They had one suspect, Ned Striker. Soon the manhunt was on. Bill C. suggested that they call a trading post in Holbrook, owned by Clarence and Mary Lee, where the Navajos liked to go and pawn. He figured that Ned needed to pawn a nice silver belt that he had. Sure enough, Ned came into the store and asked to pawn the silver belt. Mary Lee told him she didn't have the money handy and would have to go to the house for it. There, she called the sheriff, who came right away and captured Ned.

A long trial ensued, and much bickering went on about it. Eventually, Ned was sent to prison for two terms of life in Leavenworth Prison. We quite often received letters from Ned, and I still have one or two of them. In 1984, Ned was released to return home. By then he was in poor health and had decided that he loved children. I have a newspaper clipping and picture of a little granddaughter sitting on his lap. But I can never forget what he did to Charlie Mike's family.

Little Jimmy, a Navajo man who considered himself a powerful medicine man, was wizened and wrinkled like a prune. He would stand in front of the post and wheeze and groan, making all kinds of noises, claiming that he was keeping the bears away. When Bill C. expressed doubt at the claim, Little Jimmy said indignantly, "Well, there aren't any bears around, are there?" Bill had to agree his power seemed to work, as we had no bears at Wide Ruins.

Joe Toddy, father of young artist Beatien Yazz or Jimmy Toddy, had an experience with a bear. He lived at Wide Ruins until he found a wife in Canyon de Chelly and moved there with her. They had lots of small peach orchards in the canyon, and in the fall the Navajo people would gather the peaches, pit them, and spread them out on roof tops to dry. Now, a bear likes dried peaches, too, and this caused everyone some concern.

Joe had many conversations with the bear, but the creature kept coming back to steal the peaches. The Navajo do not like to kill bears and call them "brother." But they will kill them, if provoked too much. Finally, Joe felt he had to do something. He apologized to Mr. Bear but said he would have to shoot him. Joe only had a .22 rifle, so it must have been a lucky shot because he, indeed, killed the bear. Later, he admitted that to overcome any bad luck he might have from the shooting, he had removed the bear's gall bladder and eaten it. "Gosh," he said. "It sure was bitter!" Joe lived many years after that, so I guess the cure worked.

Multiple wives were fairly common in those days for the Navajo people. But one enterprising woman, Mary Ben, had two husbands—Nez Ben and John Joe Red Eye. They got along fine and took turns living with her at Wide Ruins for six months at a time. When they weren't with her, they went off to work wherever a job was available.

About the mid- to late 1940s, Bill C. and his brother Bob decided they would buy an Air Coupe plane. Bill went to Safford, Arizona, to make the purchase and fly it back. They didn't have time to buy insurance on it before a friend came out from Gallup who wanted Bill to take him for a ride. Hosteen Yazzie, an old man who mowed our runway, had piled the weeds up near the front of the plane. Bill was so excited to take his friend up, he didn't notice those clippings. When he started the engine, it sucked them up. They only rose about one to two hundred feet off the ground when the engine failed, and they started going down again. Bill didn't have a great choice. On one side there was a barbed wire fence, and on the other, an arroyo. He aimed for the arroyo, and, though the plane was a total loss, miraculously there were no injuries. Edward and I were standing there watching this whole trip. When the plane started going down, I feared that seeing his father crash would have a devastating effect on the boy. But he thought it was exciting and later became a pilot himself. I'm sure he was inspired by that brief flight.

We were Air Coupe owners only ten hours and, since the thing wasn't insured, took the full financial loss.

In 1950, Bill and Sallie Lippincott decided to sell the Wide Ruins Post to the Navajo tribe, since the reservation surrounded it by then. And we decided to move into town (Gallup) to work so our kids could go to school there. The Navajos at Wide Ruins hated to see us go, and we felt the same. But it was time to move on to our next adventure.

After we left the Wide Ruins Post, it was operated by a succession of men, both Navajo and Anglo. None of them was too successful, and it was finally closed. In the late 1970s or early 1980s, the store and living quarters burned. It's hard to believe that what was once such an active place is going back to ruins.

Jean and Ruth, circa 1946-47.

Ruth, Bill, Edward, and Jean Cousins, circa 1948.

Watermelon Time

After I got back to Wide Ruins, I was appointed to the Railroad Retirement Board. I was in charge of signing up the Indians who wanted to work on the railroad. As the Indians became unemployed, whether bumped from their jobs, lost them, or just quit their jobs to go home, they could sign up for unemployment with the railroad. But they knew that as soon as there was a job opening, they would have to go back to the railroad to work. So they would sign up every week that they were unemployed, and they would get a check. Then, when the railroad needed employees, they would call me and say, "We need forty men." I'd give the jobs to the ones who had been off the longest, rotating the work.

Ralph Jones, a Navajo, bought a wagon from me on credit and was paying a little along on it whenever he could. Then he was sent on a railroad job to Needles, California. It was midsummer and hotter than the dickens out there. I got a letter from him saying that he wanted me to buy him a herd of sheep so he could come back to the reservation and work. He wrote, "I can't live here and work any longer. This country is just like standing by a stove all day."

I wrote him with my advice: "Stay there and work. You owe me for that wagon, and I'm tired of worrying about it. If you don't pay me for it, I'll have to repossess it."

He sent a letter right back saying, "I'm sorry you're tired and worried. But that wagon is out of your hands, and I'm

Wide Ruins Post, late 1940s. Below: Corral at Wide Ruins Post.

going to pay for it. Don't you worry. I'll do the worry." And he certainly did pay for it.

Life at Wide Ruins was great. I thought I was set there for life. Jean and I had a nice home, loved country living; loved my job. We had each other, two great kids, lots of friends, enjoyed the good life. We played cards with schoolteachers in the area and later, when we ran the post ourselves, we had the swimming pool and always a big crowd on Sunday. My folks came from the ranch, friends from Gallup came out to visit, and Jean fixed nice meals for everyone. We had poker games, target practice with rifles; the women would visit; we'd have turkey shoots. There was lots of activity for such an isolated place, forty-three miles from Gallup and sixteen miles off Highway 66. Our family would go different places, exploring the countryside and sometimes have a picnic.

At the post, salesmen and repairmen would arrive by noon and sometimes stay all night, and we always enjoyed their visits. Truck drivers would arrive for lunch two or three times a week. We never had to unload freight because Indians always did it in exchange for soda pop.

When the Lippincotts took off on one of their many trips, we often wouldn't know when they'd be back. Joe Toddy, the Navajo man who worked for us at the post, generally took care of Lippincott's house while they were gone. He'd see that everything was all right, keep the fires burning and the ashes cleared, whatever needed doing around the house. He would make sure the house stayed in good shape until they got back.

One time when they were gone, Joe came running into the store, all excited. "There's an owl in the house!" he yelled. Now, the Navajos are superstitious about owls, so he wouldn't have anything to do with it. I went up to the house, and there it was, a tiny ground owl, sitting on the mantel over the fireplace. I just opened the door and let it out.

Another time when the Lippincotts were gone, Joe got into their liquor. Bill L. had a trap door in the ceiling of his library where he kept his stock of liquor, mostly scotch. You had to get a stepladder to get into it.

Bill L. was a scotch and water man. In fact, I learned to be a scotch drinker from Lippincott. When they returned from their trip, and Bill L. asked me, "Did you get into the liquor supply? It's all right, because you're perfectly welcome to it. I just want to know."

"Of course not," I answered, a little angry that he would think that. "You know I wouldn't get into it, especially without you here."

"Well, I thought so," he said. "I'm afraid Joe Toddy is getting into the booze."

"How do you know?"

"Just before I left, I opened a brand new bottle of scotch, Vat 69, and had one drink. When I got back, that bottle was almost empty."

"Well, Joe knows where it is, then," I said.

"I don't know what to do about it."

I had an idea. "Let's try this. Next time you leave, let's take that bottle of Vat 69, pour the whiskey out and put in about two inches of kerosene. Set it back, don't mention it, and see what happens." Vat 69 was a brand of Scotch that came in a dark-colored bottle, so you could replace the contents without someone suspecting it until it was opened. So, Lippincotts left on a trip. When they got back, Bill L. didn't even have to get a stepladder to see what had happened. Some of the kerosene was gone from the bottle, and a greasy spot was on the floor where the kerosene had been spat out. After that, he moved his liquor stash to a secret cellar in his office, and that ended the booze problem.

The Indian service wouldn't bring phone service to the post at Wide Ruins, only to the school for the teachers. Lippincott hired someone to put in poles and string wires, so we could have phones. Even though he paid for it, the service lines belonged to the Navajo tribe. We were connected to a party line of about six to eight families. You had a certain ring for your phone calls. To reach Gallup, your call went through Ganado, then to Window Rock, then connected to Gallup.

Many on our party line listened in on the phone calls. Dennis, a friend from Klagetoh, and I were always playing jokes on each other. He worked as a mechanic and handyman and also took care of maintenance for all the BIA day schools in the vicinity. One time, I called him and you could hear lines click. That meant someone was picking up the phone to listen. I decided to fix them and said, "I'm with the telephone company calling to check on phones in the community. I need to know the length of your receiver cord."

"About six feet."

"I'm sorry, we need the exact measurement. Have you got a tape measure?"

"Oh yes, it's exactly six feet."

"Fine. Now you can just shove it . . ." and I told him where. You could hear the phones hanging up all along the line, and he and I got a good laugh out of that one for many years.

We used to buy forty to fifty watermelons from trucks that came by the post, but we never had to unload them. The Navajos loved watermelons. They would run out and unload the whole bunch and stack them in the wareroom. They knew we'd always give them some watermelon and soda pop or something for helping.

Generally, I would put a watermelon on the counter, slice it with a knife, and tell them to help themselves. One day after unloading, I decided to try something. I'd heard that the Navajos didn't like to stab, or hurt, their food. So, I picked out a big watermelon and put it on the counter. I jabbed a knife right in the middle and left it there. "Thanks, fellows. Help yourselves!" No one touched it. By golly, they left that melon right there on the counter. I learned that they believe you should be good to your food and, in turn, it will be good to you. I put another melon on the counter, uncut, laid the knife beside it, and told them to help themselves. That time, they went to town, slicing it themselves.

The Navajos called the light bulb in a flashlight its eye or *nah*. The batteries were the heart, or *ja*. When they needed new batteries, they always wanted a new bulb, too. I told them the bulb was all right, but they said it wasn't strong enough. So I'd put in a new bulb and stash the old one on a shelf in back. The next time someone came in with a flashlight and wanted a new eye as well as a heart, I'd put that stored bulb in it. Everybody was happy with that solution.

I went into Gallup and bought a brand new 1949 Ford sedan, and all I had with it was trouble. It scooped up dust from those dirt roads like a vacuum cleaner. I took it back to Gallup to the Ford garage, and they said it needed an undersealer. I said, "Fine, but be sure every nut and bolt underneath is secure and tight." They agreed, and when I picked it up after the work was done, they said it was in top condition. I drove it back to Wide Ruins.

A few days later, on Saturday night, Jean and I and the kids headed for Chevelon Lake, where we were to meet Malin and his wife, Donna, and a friend, Tex Laughlin, to go fishing. Heck, we couldn't go over fifty miles an hour because the car shimmied so much I could hardly keep it on the road. After a nice weekend fishing, we left before the others due to the condition of the car. I knew it would take us longer to get home. We had only traveled a few miles when we could hear—and feel—a thumping on the road. I was pretty sure it was a tie rod. I took my foot off the accelerator, slowed a hundred yards or so, hit a rough spot, and went into the ditch. I couldn't find the nut to fix it, so I took the lug nut off the spare tire in the trunk, put it on the tie rod and drove into Winslow. I went to the Ford garage and told them I needed a tie rod and cotter pin. They fixed me up and we drove on to Wide Ruins.

The next day I went to the Ford garage in Gallup, parked it in front of their store, and told them I was finished with that model. When I told them what had happened, they were very apologetic. The owner of the Buick dealership, Mr. Rico Menepace, came to see me and offered to sell me a new Buick. I indicated that I was interested: "What will you give me for that Ford over there? It's brand new, with less than 1,500 miles on it."

"Brand new? What's wrong with it?"

I said, "The only good thing on that car is the radiator cap."

"Oh, it can't be that bad," he said.

"Well, look it over and tell me what kind of a deal you can come up with." He came back and said he would take it for even trade. We shook hands, and the deal was made. That Buick turned out to be a real good car.

The school at Wide Ruins did us a favor by admitting our children, but it wasn't adequate for them. Their students were Navajo children, and they taught mostly English. We decided to send Edward and Ruth to the school at Klagetoh, eight miles away, and I drove them twice a day. I hated to make that trip over such a bad road as the one to Klagetoh, so I started looking for an older car. It just happened that on the day I went into town to buy the 1949 Ford, I spotted a 1929 Model A Roadster. I decided to buy it to use as a school car for the poor roads to Klagetoh. The Model A needed some repairs, and it had a bad cylinder head plus a few other parts. I had to send to Sears mail order for the Model A parts, because nobody had any more parts for that car in Gallup. It was an easy car to work on; even though I wasn't a mechanic, I could fix it. But I continued having trouble with it and finally sold it to a man at Klagetoh Trading Post. He drove that Model A to Chicago, kept it for many years, and never had any more trouble with it.

I decided that I should learn to fly a plane. I would go into Gallup real early in the mornings two or three times a week to take lessons. When I finished seven hours of dual training, I soloed. After forty hours of regular flying, as well as practicing stalls and spins, I took the test ride and passed. I became a private pilot, which meant I could take passengers, but not for pay.

I rented a horse pasture from Hosteen Yazzie, hung a rag on a stick for a windsock, and we had our airport. Then I spent all of my savings and bought a new Air Coupe. It was a beautiful plane, but I wrecked the thing before I got to enjoy it much. We didn't get hurt, but it totaled the Air Coupe.

In those days, you could rent a Piper Cub for five dollars an hour. All the Indians at Wide Ruins wanted to go for rides. I'd get the airplane off ground and up to cruising speed, hold it level and straight, and let them take over controls so they could say they'd flown an airplane. Of course, anybody can fly it after it leaves ground, and it only takes a second to straighten it out if anything goes wrong. One Navajo, Ralph Jones, climbed up to three thousand feet and circled his hogan, then flew over the painted desert, the petrified forest, and the black petrified forest, which is near Wide Ruins. When we turned to go back home, I noticed his shoulders twitching and thought he must be getting a little nervous and tight. So I came took over and landed it. Later, I asked him if he was nervous. He said, "I was a little scared, but after we landed, I was just happy that I got to fly a plane."

One day I drove my automobile to the landing strip at Wide Ruins. There was a sandy place before the bridge, and I got stuck in the sand. I was trying to dig it out, when John Joe came along in his pickup truck. He got two Navajo friends and some heavy planks. Those men laid down on their backs and jacked the car and put it on planks. I was then able to back out of there. I was grateful and asked, "How much do I owe you?"

"Nothing," they said. "You wouldn't have charged us."

"Well, that's right," I admitted. "I would have done it for you. Thanks." That's the way it was, the way we made it out there, by helping each other.

In the fall of 1948 at Wide Ruins, a fellow named Drefkoff began working for the Navajo tribe and got things all stirred up. Some thought he was red. He claimed the trading posts were cheating the Indians and paying them less than the value of the wool and rugs. He wanted the tribe to take over all the trading posts and brought charges against the traders that were ridiculous and false. Sallie and Bill Lippincott and some other traders got together and went to a Senate hearing in Washington, D.C., along with the senators from New Mexico and Arizona.

Drefkoff was proven wrong in his allegations and left the reservation. For a while, we thought everything was settled and doing all right again. We didn't think much more about the incident. Everything seemed secure after the traders proved to the Senate that the charges were false. But the seed had been planted to the Indians, and the Navajo tribe wanted to take over the place at Wide Ruins.

The way we did business at Wide Ruins, we sold the rugs that we bought from the Navajos for only a small 10 percent profit. We bought clean, dry wool from them and figured if we could get our cost out of it, we were happy. Everybody else was trying to do the same thing. If wool was twenty-five cents a pound, we paid twenty-five cents a pound in cash, not trade.

The Wide Ruins Trading Post sat on 160 acres of deeded land, and Lippincott had the clear title. The Navajo tribe wanted it, and other trading posts, mainly for the land. By then, the post was surrounded by the reservation. Given all the problems of the time, few people wanted to go into the trading business, so Lippincott agreed to sell it to the tribe. He got what he asked, and more than an ordinary trader could have paid, but still didn't get what it was truly worth, by any means. The post at that time was nice property with a beautiful home, a manager's home and a guest house. We had a thousand-gallon butane tank that was buried, so there were no eyesores at the post.

If Lippincott had stayed, we could have made a profit, but it would have been tough. The tribal government wanted to examine the books and charge a sales tax, thus increasing the costs of everything. The state didn't even charge sales tax on the reservation at that time. Lippincott wouldn't have anything to do with business that way, so he told the Navajos they could buy the Wide Ruins Post in the spring of 1950. The Indians were supposed to take ownership of the trading post on August 1, 1950.

The Lippincotts didn't feel too badly about it. They thought if the Indians could swing it, they should have the trading post and keep it going. But the Indians never made much of a profit, as far as I know.

At the time of the sale, the tribal leaders asked if I'd run it for them. I told them, "Yes, I'm interested because I don't have job. How much would you pay?" Well, the wages were so ridiculously low that I couldn't make a living for my family. I told them I'd need "stealing privileges" from the store to make ends meet; otherwise, I couldn't take it. Of course, I was joking, but the truth was, there was no way I could make it on

Bill Cousins, age forty.

the amount of money they offered. So I turned down the job at Wide Ruins.

There I was, forty years of age with no job, no money, no home, and a family to support. I didn't know what to do. My brother Tom offered me a job working in his hardware store in Gallup. I agreed to go to work for him at Hart Hardware.

We had no place to live in Gallup. I wanted to buy a house because I felt that renting was pouring money down a rat hole. A friend, Frank Burke, worked in the contracting business as well as the insurance business and offered to build me a three-bedroom house for approximately thirteen thousand dollars. Now, that was quite a bit of money, but it would have been a nice home in a good locality. I talked to Bill Lippincott about it, and he knew of two houses for sale in one of the better areas in Gallup. They were beautiful homes for eighteen thousand dollars. He said, "Why don't you pick out one of them, I'll pay for it, and you can pay me for it any way you want to." Eighteen thousand dollars was an insurmountable amount of money, and I just couldn't handle it. Now, I realize that I should have done it, because I ended up spending much more than that, plus all my labor, on the house I eventually bought.

Another friend called from Gallup and told me he'd found a house in a nice locality and sitting on a lot and a half. He said it was small and may need some work. But the price was only $4,900. So, I tore off to Gallup and went up to the house at 206 E. Maple. The owner, a high school teacher moving to Albuquerque, said, "Come on in and I'll show it to you."

"I don't need to see inside," I said. "All I want to do is look underneath it." I scooted into the crawl space under the house and saw that it needed a foundation repair. I knew I could fix it, so I said, "I'll take it." Fortunately, Jean trusted my judgment, because she never saw it before I bought it.

I went down to the bank, paid a thousand dollars down, and took the rest on payments. I finally did go and look at the inside. It was small, but nice, and I knew it would be fine for us. But the darned thing faced east instead of Maple Street. I already had ideas on how I could remodel it.

MacGregor, the scottie dog, Bill, and Ruth.

The deal was consummated, and I took over the house. It was getting close to July 1, and the teacher and his family weren't quite ready to move out. "That's all right," I said. "I have work at Wide Ruins."

About July 10, Tom came out to Wide Ruins to see me. "I need you at the store real bad," he said.

"I can't leave the post until the Lippincotts turn it over to the tribe, because I have to inventory," I explained. "I have to take care of the job here."

"Couldn't Jean do that?"

"Well, yes." Jean was a fine trader, and I had no doubts that she could do it. When I talked to the Lippincotts, they said it would be okay for me to go on to work in Gallup if I'd come back to inventory when they turned it over to the tribe on August 1. I agreed to do that. On the fifteenth of July, 1950, I moved into town, leaving my family at Wide Ruins.

I would work at the store all day, then go to my house and "batch." I'd cook my supper, then start working on that house, a little at a time. I didn't do much on the inside because I was waiting for Jean to move in and give me her opinions. On Saturday evenings after work, I'd drive one and a half hours to Wide Ruins to spend the weekend with my family. On Monday morning at 7:30 AM, I'd be back in Gallup working at the hardware store, leaving Jean to run the post.

This temporary arrangement was satisfactory with everybody. Jean knew everything I did about trading. In fact, she was one of the best traders I'd ever seen. She worked well with the Navajos. They liked her, and she liked them, which was absolutely necessary in that business.

Lippincott bought a big truck to move his furniture and all his things to northern California, where he was going into the cattle business. He offered to move our household into Gallup, so we loaded up the truck. By then, we had lots of stuff—nice furniture, wooden beds, all the kids' things, and a gas refrigerator. We couldn't take Ruth's kitty, because he wouldn't get in the car. And neither would our dog, Roosevelt. That darned dog came to our house as a stray, nothing but skin bones, and stayed. I called him Roosevelt because I couldn't get rid of Franklin D. Roosevelt, and I couldn't get rid of that dog. We fed him, and he stayed around but wouldn't come into the house and was afraid of the car. I hated to leave both animals, so I paid a Navajo friend five dollars to take care of them. We took MacGregor, our scottie dog, who loved Gallup and lived to a ripe old age.

The Navajos at Wide Ruins hated to see Jean and me move, and we were sad to leave. They liked us and the Lippincotts, and many of us are still friends today.

This was life on a reservation trading post, around the 1930s and 1940s. That was our life, to deal with the situations that Indians and traders presented. Everything was pertinent to your job as a trader. You had to know and care about the Indians' lives. The Navajos were great people to deal with. We all enjoyed them. Jean liked the Navajo people more than anyone I've ever known. So, with a few regrets, we headed to Gallup for a different kind of business.

Gallup Business

Jean explains details of the business and the growth of Indian arts and crafts as a profitable endeavor for both the Navajo and the trader. As she moved toward independence, Jean dealt effectively with forms of harassment in her own way. Even though she established herself as an entrepreneur and businesswoman, she couldn't obtain a loan because of prejudicial feelings toward women entrepreneurs at that time in Gallup. Owning her own business, a personal goal for many years, had to be postponed.

Bill's integrity and business sense were further tested and developed. He remained the jokester and storyteller, loving life and customers, and holding steadfastly to his family.

Snap Decision

We moved into Gallup and I decided to become a housewife for the first time in my life. But I soon found that boring after the exciting times trading. Bill was working with his brother, Tom Cousins, in his store, Hart Hardware and Plumbing Company, and had committed to help him.

So, when Asa Glascock wanted Bill to come work for him in his store, the Glascock Trading Post, Bill refused. "But I know a good Indian trader. The best, in fact."

"Yeah? Who?"

"My wife, Jean."

Well, Asa was reluctant to hire a woman, but agreed to give me a try. I was so proud of me! And I felt very honored that Bill had recommended me. In January, I went for the job interview. I had never worked for anyone on an actual payroll. Oh, I had worked at the posts but never got any money for it. But I had learned well from an excellent teacher, my husband, Bill. He had instructed me in the way Navajos felt and thought about things, and the ways they preferred to do business. So I went to see Asa Glascock with confidence as well as a little trepidation.

The first thing he asked me was, "How much do you want an hour?"

I had never experienced working outside the post and didn't know about minimum wage laws. Very timidly I asked, "Would thirty cents an hour be too much?"

He threw up his hands in horror. "My God, woman, I couldn't hire anybody for thirty cents an hour! The minimum wage is seventy-five, and that's what I'll start you out with."

To me, that was great! I thought I had found a fortune. I had, in lots of ways, because Asa was an astute businessman and he had built up this beaded belt business on his own. From R. M. Bruchman in Winslow we bought beaded moccasins and plain leather belts. We issued beads to the Indians, they made the bead strips and brought them back to us. Then we sewed the strips onto the leather belts, thus making the beaded belts ourselves. We sold the Indian beaded belts to all the park services in the U.S. and Alaska and shipped them regularly. That was quite an enterprise in itself.

For trade, we bought from the Indians beaded cow heads (made from sheep's vertebrae). Some of those Zuni women were quite creative at sewing the beaded faces on those things. They made three kinds of fully beaded rabbit's feet creations: an Indian woman wearing a full, colorful skirt; an Indian chief with a brightly colored, fancy headdress; and a cowboy wearing trousers. The Indians made enough money from these items to pick up a sack of flour, baking powder, a can of tomatoes, and necessities of that sort.

The bead department was at one end of the store where Asa had a long counter, about twelve feet long by three feet wide, lined with ten-quart water buckets filled with seed beads imported from Czechoslovakia in every color of the rainbow. At the tail end of the counter, we had a bucket of mixed beads, where you could get all colors at once. They sold for twenty-five cents a shot glass.

In five to six months after starting to work for Asa, I was completely in charge of the Glascock Trading Post. He and his wife traveled back to their home state of Missouri or to Tennessee, where they had another shop in Gatlinburg.

Every time Asa found property he liked, he would call me long distance and ask how much money was in the bank. I would inform him, then send him a check for the amount if he wanted it.

I was careful not to send all the money, because I knew we had beads, leather, and lacing to pay for, as well as other merchandise. All these things kept the business going. The leather belts were made in Tennessee or Georgia, tailored and ready to accommodate a Western buckle. The lacing was a plastic decorative strip that the Indian women sewed on the belts.

It was my job to keep the payroll record straight on who had materials out, who had returned the work, and who hadn't. So, my responsibilities grew as the business grew. Fortunately, I was able to handle it all. I learned a lot during those times, and it was a great joy for me to be able to feel like I was earning my money.

Asa was extremely generous. Every so often he would come by and say, "You'd better take a ten cents an hour raise, retroactive to so-and-so date."

That was wonderful to me. When Bill and I moved into town, we had a lot of repair work to do on the house in order to make it livable. At Christmas that first year, Asa gave me a five-hundred-dollar bonus. What a surprise! Bill was able to get busy working on the house. We added two bedrooms and did all necessary repairs.

Every Saturday in the store, we packed what we called our "lunches." These were paper sacks of beads with the colors marked on the outside. We would hand these sacks of beads out to the Navajo women when they came into town on Saturdays to sell their bead strips. We gave them another sack of beads on a consignment basis. When they returned beadwork the next week, they got credit for the sack of beads and received another bag. That kept the work going.

The Zuni people also came in the store to buy beads for their beaded projects. In many ways, they were much more enterprising than the Navajo. But we had to watch them carefully, because some had sticky fingers. They wore black manta dresses, off one shoulder and cinched at the waist with a belt. When we weren't looking, they would reach down and scoop up a handful of beads and drop them into the front of their dresses. They would get away fast. But no one was willing to check them anyway.

The Zunis made tiny beaded dolls out of rabbit's feet. We called them Comanches (Indian man with headdress), Men (like cowboys), and Skirts (women). The Zunis had frequent dances. Day or night, they would dance for anything—rain, sun, new house, healing, everything. I was often invited and wanted to go to the Shalako dance, but Bill refused, so I had to settle with watching the street dances at the Gallup Ceremonial.

Along with the beaded belt products we sold to the national parks were little red cedar hatchets carved from the cedar trees which were in abundance around Gallup. The children liked those, and we sold them for twenty-five cents. We also had Indian-made bows and arrows which sold for seventy-five cents.

During the winter, business was slow. We sent out requests for orders so we could fill and pack them according to an assigned winter shipping date. That kept us busy during the slow seasons.

I studied the Dun and Bradstreet book that gathered financial ratings like it was the Bible. Everyone with a G rating was sent a form letter asking for their business, for that meant they had good credit and were reliable. Many times our efforts paid off and we would get an order, because we always had a G rating.

Asa's wife often went back to Gatlinburg, Tennessee, where she had a gift shop. One time she returned with a beaded necklace that had a little doll in the center done in beadwork. The Navajo women who worked for us studied those necklaces and somehow figured out how to do them. The Glascocks had about a hundred of them made up and sent them to our good customers, asking if they would be interested in an order of these necklaces during the winter. We had great response to that and filled many orders for them.

After another visit to Tennessee in the early 1950s, Mrs. Glascock brought back the first bolo tie that I had ever seen. We asked our silversmiths if they could make some of those, and they did. So we had our first production of the popular Western bolo ties.

In general, Asa was a good employer, most generous, and very forgiving. Every time I made a mistake, he would say, "Well, we're going to have to send you back to school." That was just enough incentive to make me remember not to make that mistake again.

One of the things I felt most badly about was, once I filled an order for one of our best customers in Grand Rapids. But instead of putting Michigan on the address, I sent it to Grand Rapids, Minnesota. A few months later, a letter came asking why they had not received their order. I retraced my steps and discovered my mistake. By then we couldn't recover the order, and Asa just said, "Send it again to the right address this time." I felt terrible, but what could I do? I sent the order out again. Asa never mentioned it again.

Finally, Asa and his wife decided they would like to retire back in Hannibal, Missouri. Asa offered to sell the shop to me. I was honored and wanted to buy it. But Bill and I couldn't raise the money, because no bank in town would loan the money to a woman at that time.

I had worked for Asa about eight years and was sorry to see him leave. Also, I hated to lose my good job. The new owners asked me to stay on, but they wouldn't meet my price. By that time, I thought I was pretty important in the business. Obviously they didn't think I was that important.

I wasn't out of work very long. A friend across town heard that I was leaving Asa's store and asked me if I was interested in working in his curio shop. M. L. Woodard ran one of the most elite shops in Gallup, Woodard's Indian Arts and Crafts. I told him I would be happy to work there. M. L. was a fine man and a very astute businessman. I learned so much from him about the trading business that I was able to use in our businesses later. During this time, I just never seemed to stop growing and learning.

I worked for M. L. about five or six years. I liked him all right as a boss, and he was usually good to me. The main thing I disliked about him was that he would write my paycheck and carry it around in his pocket for a few days. As a result, I would never get my money on time and would have to ask for it. I guess you would say that it was a form of harassment, but I learned to live with it. For a while.

"Oh, I'm sorry," he'd say, as if he just forgot about my paycheck. But I knew that he did it purposely to make me ask. It was important for me to get my money on time. We had two kids in school and were pretty strapped during those years. Often I didn't even have ten cents for a coffee break.

The shop was called Woodard's Indian Arts and Crafts Shop, and we sold only Indian-made products. But everything was of excellent quality, only top-grade merchandise: pottery, silver, paintings, rugs, the whole ball of wax. Our goods generally took grand prize or blue ribbon at the Gallup Intertribal Ceremonial, so they were considered fine art.

One year in June, the Lions Club held a parade on Cole Avenue in Gallup, and Bill was riding in it. In all my life, I had never seen Bill on horseback, and I wanted to see him. He was so tall that I was curious to see how far down his legs came, or if they touched the ground. (They didn't!) There was nobody in the shop, so, along with everyone else, I stood in front of the store on the sidewalk so I could see the parade. When the tail end of the parade came along, I went back into the store with some customers coming behind me. There was M. L. Woodard in the back of the store, snapping his fingers at me to get back to work. I'm sure my red hair stood on end. The more I thought about it, the madder I got.

I went home to lunch and told Bill all about it. I complained angrily that M. L. had snapped his fingers at me and I didn't like that one bit. Finally I shut up, and Bill said, "Jean, you don't need that job. You can quit, you know."

After stewing on that awhile, I went back to work and approached my boss: "Mr. Woodard, I quit. I'm giving you my notice now."

He looked so surprised. "But what happened?"

"Well, in all my life I've never had anybody snap their fingers at me and tell me to get busy. You know that I'm a good worker, and don't need somebody snapping me along."

He fell all over himself apologizing. "I didn't mean it that way. I'm real sorry."

"It doesn't make any difference. I'm going to leave you. I will stay for the Ceremonial, but that's all." The annual Gallup Ceremonial was about two months away. "After that, I'm gone." M. L. was very apologetic, but it was too late because I was too upset by the whole affair. So, I went back to Hart

Hardware and Plumbing Company and worked for Bill and Tom for about six months. Then another offer came along.

A good friend, Tobe Turpen, Jr., approached us and said we had been recommended to him by a mutual friend, Carl Hine, to run a pawn shop in partnership with him. Would I be interested in running it and possibly putting the shop in the hardware store? The proposition excited me, but I knew I had to get permission. "That's not up to me, but up to Tom and Bill," I answered. When I asked them, they said readily that it would be fine. Might even improve their business. Our part of the bargain was to build a fireproof vault to take care of the jewelry in stock and pawn, which we agreed to do.

Only our names were on the contract, Jean and Bill Cousins and Tobe Turpen. I was thrilled. Our silent partner, Mr. Turpen, started me out in the Indian jewelry business with ten thousand dollars, and I opened my own shop, Jean's Jewelry, in February of 1961. I thought that was great and was so pleased with my new business. I figured I had done all right. Since I had not put up any money or anything, the deal was more in my favor than his, because he made me a 60/40 proposition: At the end of the year, we split the profits with 60 percent for us and 40 percent for Mr. Turpen. It turned out very well.

I learned as much as I could about jewelry, studying John Adair's book on old-fashioned jewelry, *The Navajo and Pueblo Silversmiths,* from beginning to end, and used it as my reference book. I managed to get the silversmiths who came to my shop to make particular pieces of jewelry that the run-of-the-mill curio store didn't have in stock. That paid off handsomely, and soon we developed some unique, well-made jewelry.

I started, little by little, buying handmade silver from some of the Navajos. Through this, I built up quite a nice inventory of jewelry to sell to go along with what Mr. Turpen had given me on consignment. When I sold those pieces and paid them off, he would supply me more. Eventually I had quite a good stock of nice Indian jewelry, and a solid business of clients. Jean's All-Indian Jewelry and Pawn Shop became one of the better jewelry stores in Gallup. We were small and modest, but I dealt only with the old, traditional-style Navajo jewelry and very little Zuni at that time.

Pawn shops in that area were an integral part of the Indians' lives. They functioned as banks to the Navajos and Zunis. We had customers who kept their jewelry in our vault, much as we might use a safety deposit box in a bank.

We came to know our Indian clients well. They and members of their families were individuals and friends, not just customers. As with anyone else, sometimes they found themselves short of cash. The beautiful and not so beautiful jewels were put in pawn with us. The amounts we could loan were limited and tied to fair market prices. On special occasions, such as their social events, we would loan them their jewelry to wear, even if they were still paying on it. The silver and turquoise they wore represented their financial status.

When pawned, the jewels became their bank account. Like anyone else, they occasionally lost the bank account, but not without first being given numerous notices and every opportunity to redeem their pawn. We charged interest which was tightly regulated by law, and we always notified customers when their time was running short. Often we would hold some of their family jewelry as long as a year after their pawn time had run out. We held it even longer if they were making an effort to pay.

We did not like selling the "dead pawn" to the curio dealers or even to Anglos. Nor did we like the Diné to redeem it for burials. In either case, that piece of jewelry either left the country of its origin or went underground. Thus, many of the earliest and more beautiful pieces disappeared. Strangely enough, some of the pawn that went to local dealers quite often showed up at various places to be sold again. Some even filtered its way back home again. I was once given a beautiful Pima Indian basket that had been retrieved from a trash pile on the East Coast.

The big showcase in my store had long trays of jewelry that we could pull out and put in the vault at night. One evening, we forgot to put them in the safe, and that was the night we were robbed. The guilty one turned out to be a white man whose last name was Ambler and who worked for the Gallup Police Department as a dispatcher. It seems that Ambler had a gang of thieves and would dispatch the police to one end of town while they robbed businesses on the other end. One night when he was with them, the police had somehow been tipped off to their plans and waited in a stakeout at the Navajo Chevrolet garage. While the gang was breaking into the safe, the police came to arrest them. Ambler whirled and shot to death one of the officers, and the other officers shot and killed him.

After our robbery, Tom's wife, Hazel, came by the store to see what happened to the jewelry and said, "You know, you're going to have to pay for all that."

Bill was furious. "You bet we will, but we don't owe you for it. We owe the man who let us have the jewelry to sell. Furthermore, you have no claim to that pawn and jewelry store. That's Jean's. So you have no need to worry about it." Bill was so mad because there was a bit of history between them, as there is in all families. When we first moved to Gallup, Bill went to work for his older brother, Tom, in his hardware store. Tom was in ill health and nearing retirement and was struggling to keep the doors of the store open. So we remortgaged our home several times and put the money into the hardware store to keep it going. Under those circumstances, there certainly wasn't money for a salary for Bill. So we lived on the proceeds of our pawn and jewelry business. Eventually, Tom and Hazel retired to Wickenburg and left Bill in charge of the hardware store. Hazel was a strange person, and since Tom was very ill with diabetes, we did most of our communicating with her. We heard from various friends that she would call the businesses "our pawn shop" and "our jewelry shop," referring to themselves. We paid rent to them for our portion of the building that we used for the pawn shop. So, after all our hard work for them, we were quite upset by her attitude.

Well, poor Tom passed on. We wanted to buy the hardware store from Hazel, but she said she didn't think she wanted to sell it to us. And that after Bill had worked for her more than seven years without any wages and put his money into their store. Hazel finally sold the building but could not get a buyer for the merchandise. We bought the hardware stock from her, and in 1971 we opened our own store, Cousins Hardware and Indian Jewelry, in a different location, at 304 W. 66 Avenue (old Route 66) in Gallup.

We devised a perpetual type of inventory and bookkeeping so that at the end of every day we knew how much we had taken in and how much had gone out. Even other shops used this system and adapted it to their businesses. Pawn shops and Indian traders still use it today. During those years of working in Gallup, we had many happy days, and made some fine friends. We appreciated and enjoyed our Indian customers.

Some colorful characters:
A Navajo medicine man named Charley Hale came in one day with quite a large, old-fashioned trunk. He wanted to

pawn it for two hundred dollars. Well, that was quite a sum in those days, and I said, "I'll have to look inside the trunk and see what's in there first."

Charley refused. "No, you can't do that."

"Then we can't loan you money on it."

"You can trust me," he said. "I'll be back for it."

After I had a consultation with Bill, we decided to take a chance. This old man was funny. He was almost blind, had to have people lead him in and out of the store, and interpret for him. He always wore his bifocal glasses upside down.

We went ahead and pawned the chest. The old man put a padlock on it and kept the keys himself. He came back now and then to check on it, didn't want to take it, but just wanted make sure it was in safekeeping.

Bill had intentions of making a key that would open the trunk so we could see what was in it and if we had a worthless pig in a poke or whatever. But he couldn't make a key for that particular lock, so we never saw inside until Charlie opened it himself. Eventually, within his allotted time for the pawn, Charlie Hale came back to redeem his chest. Bill persuaded him to show us what was in it. We were so curious we could pop. He unlocked it and opened the lid.

Lo and behold, there were cougar skins, silver bridles, silver belts, turquoise beads, old handwoven baskets, buckskins, anything a medicine man would need to help him along. When the old man passed on, his children divided the contents among them. What treasures they had!

Henry Curley was a funny, little bitty sawed-off guy who spoke a little pidgin English, Navajo scattered with English. He would always come into the shop and introduce himself all around by saying, "I'm Henry Curley. You know me— Henry Curley."

Yes, I would think. I know you, Henry, sometimes only too well. Every time he got his Social Security check, he would come into town and head straight for the hardware store, asking if we would cash it.

"Well, yes, sure, we'll cash it."

He took ten dollars to spend and wanted to purchase some things with the rest. He would buy a hammer, a bucket, ax, or whatever caught his eye, but he would want to leave his items there for a short time. A few days later he would come back and say, "I don't need that hammer. Can I trade it in for cash?"

"Yes." And we would give him the cash.

That strange process went on until he had all his money back, and he would go on a rip-roaring drunk. My, my, old Henry Curley was funny. We never did figure him out, but we sure remembered him.

One of my Navajo customers had a very Jewish name, Alan Rosenberg. "How did you get your name?" I asked.

"Some damn schoolteacher gave it to me when I was a kid," he answered. This practice was typical. Many Navajo children had names the teachers couldn't pronounce, so they named them something else. Alan Rosenberg's widow is still a customer of Ruth today.

Francisco Nez was wrinkled as a prune and straight and stiff as an arrow. He had a bladder problem, though, and we could hardly stand to get close to him because of the urine smell. The first of every month, he brought in a beautiful string of coral beads to pawn. Then some time during that month, he would take them out of pawn. He always had all his little grandkids hanging on him with their hands out, and he was very generous with them. At the beginning of the month, he was back to pawn his coral beads. His business was like a revolving door, always coming back around.

Mary Hubble (not related to the Hubbells of Ganado) was a very good, hard-drinking Navajo woman. She had a single strand of turquoise beads and was always in financial trouble, so she would pawn those beads. Her son would come in to the store and redeem the beads and beg her not to do it again. He also asked her not to drink anymore. She answered by saying, "Your ass sure is on fire; you use *your* money to buy dog food." She disapproved of her son buying dog food for his dogs, thinking that was wasteful. I guess she felt they could eat scraps or fend for themselves.

We tried to keep some old interesting merchandise as well as some new things. We had an old-fashioned hardware store and wanted to keep it in that style. Our daughter, Ruth, lived in Dallas at the time and would scour antique shops for old coffee mills, cabbage cutters, and—would you believe it—Log Cabin syrup cans. Those old cans were some of our best sellers.

One day, I saw an advertisement in the paper where an Amish family in Iowa had buggy whips for sale. Bill thought that would be a keen thing to have in the store, so I wrote to the address in Iowa. Finally, we received the buggy whips. They were beautiful leatherwork. Then we got the idea that we would like a buggy to go along with these whips. From the same family, we negotiated to buy an old-fashioned buggy at a magnificent price, about two hundred dollars plus shipping charges. We waited with bated breath for that buggy to get here. But, a long, long time passed, and it didn't arrive.

Desperate to find our buggy, we flew to Waterloo, Iowa, and rented a taxi to take us out to the Amish farm. There, in the family barn, sat the buggy we had bought. The Amish man, Mr. Yoder, had tried to ship it but didn't know how to crate it. The truck line wouldn't accept it without the proper crating. But he failed to let us know that.

So Bill helped him build a crate and paid more money to ship it. When the buggy finally arrived in Gallup, it was in pieces because they'd had to take it apart to ship it. First thing we did was to reupholster it and put it back together. Soon it was just like new and looked so fine. We put the buggy in the big front window of the hardware store. We were located right on Highway 66 near a traffic light. Folks would have to stop at the red light or for trains that would block traffic, so they would get to see that buggy while they were sitting there. When the light changed, often they would go around the block and come into the store to get a good look at our buggy. That way we drew a lot of curious customers. The buggy was a good form of advertisement. Another way we advertised was through an almanac calendar that we gave to customers. They really like those. At other times we would put Aunt Lois's poem, "A Navajo Sandpainting," in the newspaper, especially for the Ceremonial. When we liquidated our business many years later, our old-fashioned buggy that took so much time and effort to bring to Gallup was the first thing to sell.

We kept the pawn shop in our store, Cousins Hardware and Indian Jewelry, and Bill and I worked together through 1978. At that time, we moved the pawn and jewelry shop to another location at the east end of Gallup, 2000 E. 66 Avenue, where my daughter still maintains the shop. I'll be eternally grateful to Mr. Turpen for giving me my business start.

In 1980 we retired to Concho, Arizona, to fish, play golf, and have fun. It was a beautiful place to live.

Poem written by Bill Cousins's Aunt Lois and used to advertise at ceremonial time.

Dry Paint

When we got to Gallup, Jean began putting things in place, making a home. While she was at it, she found all the problems with the house. The septic tank didn't drain well, the gas line leaked, and the electricity was a big fire hazard. I completely replaced the gas lines and had no more leaks.

The next problem to tackle was the electrical wiring, which was a series of extension cords around the house that were so bad they had scorched the walls. It was truly a dangerous situation. A friend and I rewired the entire place, putting in new outlets and new ceiling lights.

A neighbor came by trying to get our street incorporated into the city of Gallup. I gave him a twenty-five-dollar donation, and we were able to get a sewer line running to the house which I dug myself. After that, we had no more problems with the septic tank.

I added on two bedrooms, a hall, and two closets. After working all day at the hardware store, I would come home at night, mix up a batch of mortar, and lay eight to twelve blocks, working until dark. Jean was right by my side; she was always there when the chips were down.

Then we tore out a partition, and made a sixteen- by twenty-four-foot living room with a picture window and the front door facing north toward Maple Street. We resealed the ceiling, reconstructed the foundation with cement, stuccoed all the walls, and added a new front porch. Next, we built a

House on Maple Street prior to remodeling. Below: House on Maple Street after remodeling, with front facing the street.

two-car garage, a small workshop on the back, and a private bedroom for Edward which, years later, I turned into my workshop. I completely turned that little house around.

We made a nice lawn and a patio with a roof over part of it, so you wouldn't get wet if it rained while you had a picnic lunch. Jean loved gardening and had beautiful flowers, especially tulips. She directed the planting of trees and rose bushes in our yard and even built a vegetable garden out back. I put plastic pipes with holes under the soil, so all you had to do was turn on the spigot to water the garden. She raised tomatoes, squash, and other vegetables, which we all enjoyed very much. It was real nice and a long way from the hogan we'd first moved into at Wide Ruins.

We finally sold the house in 1981 for eighty thousand dollars, and it still stands today. Of course, we were working and improving it the full time we lived there, putting in many hours and about sixty thousand dollars altogether, but it was all a labor of love.

The hardware business was completely new to me. I knew a little about it because I'd sold some tools in the post, but this was different. It took a while to learn where everything was located in the store. Also, I was used to dealing with Navajos, not Anglos. The Navajos generally would buy only one thing at a time, pay cash, get their change, then choose something else until they bought all they wanted or ran out of money. If they wanted a sack of flour, you'd get it for them, they would pay, you would give them change, then maybe they'd want a can of coffee. This was probably due to their lack of knowledge in dealing with money. It's not so prevalent today. Also, Navajos generally knew what they wanted and would look over the merchandise and choose. Anglos, on the other hand, often asked for your advice and comparisons of brands, prices, and uses. Then you would total it all up and give one bill either for cash or credit.

The bookkeeper at Hart Hardware, Tilly, would check the cash register out every night before she went home at five o'clock. Sometimes we stayed open until 6:30 or 7:00, so all those sales went onto the next day's business. One morning, soon after I arrived there, she and Tom had quite a long conversation, with both of them occasionally looking over towards me. I tried to ignore them, but I felt uneasy and wondered what in the world was going on. Finally, Tom came over to me and said, "Look, we sold a 30.06 Winchester rifle. There was a cash ticket made out, dated yesterday, but the money isn't in the register. Can you explain what happened?"

I said, "Well, you caught me. I must have put the money in my pocket."

"Aw, come on, you didn't do that. What happened?"

"The only other thing that could have happened is that I made that sale after 5:30 PM last night and it's on today's register tape. Did you check it?"

"No." He went back to the cash register and checked. "Yep, you're right. Here it is." Both of them were red-faced and apologetic. After that, there wasn't ever any question about my honesty. Later, I changed that practice of closing the sales at five o'clock, so we started out from scratch every morning.

Charlie Hengle was the custodian at one of the schools. He, too, was a tough nut to deal with and always giving me little problems. I just did the best I could with him because we needed the school business. One hot, summer day he came in and announced, "I want to borrow the scaffolding." Several plumbers worked for us, and they had scaffolding at the store that was thirty to forty feet high.

"Okay," I said.

Charlie backed his truck into the alley and loaded the scaffolding from the back door. Meantime, someone parked in the alley so he couldn't get out. He began fussing and fuming, raising the dickens because he was all blocked in. Finally I said, "Just forget about it. You can't get out until they leave. I'm sure they'll be out in a little bit after they unload for the California market. Come with me and I'll show you what we do when things like that happen." So I led him out the back to the bar next door, which was run by a great fellow named Johnny Mehelcich. We sat at the bar, and I ordered Charlie a big mug of beer. I had a Coke because I was working and didn't want beer on my breath. From then on, Charlie Hengle was my friend. He would come down to the store every night about closing time so we could go to the bar and have a beer.

Soon after I started working in Gallup, Mr. Asa Glascock came to the store and tried to hire me to come and work for him in his post in Gallup. "Sorry, I'm committed to this job and helping Tom," I said.

"Well, do you know of anyone who could help me?"

"I know one of the best," I said.

"Who?"

"My wife, Jean."

He seemed a little reluctant but agreed to give her a try. Jean worked successfully for him for several years and he developed complete trust in her. When he decided to retire, he offered to sell the post to Jean. But at that time, we couldn't raise the money and the banks wouldn't loan to a woman. So, she worked in the hardware store for a few months until a better offer came along.

Eventually, Jean and I went into the jewelry and pawn business in the Hart Hardware building in the late fifties. Since Tom's sight was going bad, and we wanted to help him, we turned all profits back into the hardware store during the first year. After that first year, we decided it was our business and ran it separately.

My brother Tom didn't stay at the hardware store much because he liked to play golf. I became more and more involved with running the store. He came to me one day and said, "I'm going to retire and leave town. We're moving to Arizona. You'll have to run the store."

"Okay. I'm not exactly anxious to do that, but if that's what you want, I'll do it."

Tom and Hazel bought land just outside Wickenburg, Arizona, and built a beautiful home. Tom played golf and really enjoyed his retirement until his eyes started bothering him, and he was diagnosed to have diabetes. They put him on insulin, but his eyesight continued to be very bad. I offered to take no salary in an effort to save the business because Tom was my brother and he was going blind.

Tom and Hazel turned the management of the hardware over to me but continued to draw salaries just as they had when they were still working there. The store also paid many of their expenses, such as country club dues and large automobile expenses, like insurance. The store even bought them a new Cadillac. Well, it didn't take long for the hardware to be in bad financial shape with little cash on hand.

Until they moved to Wickenburg, the business was known as Hart Hardware and Plumbing Company. When they left, they decided to discontinue the plumbing, which was a mistake because the plumbing part of the business was very profitable. By closing it out, the profits were much less. We found it impossible to survive on just hardware. I wanted to add the plumbing back, but Hazel absolutely refused to allow me to do that. She could not realize that the plumbing was profitable because during the coldest winter months of January, February, and March, it cost a lot to pay the plumbers' salaries and keep them on the payroll. She couldn't believe that the profits for the rest of the year more than made up for those months.

A few years later, Tom went to a hospital in Phoenix with a blood clot in his leg. They operated but didn't get it all. The next morning after operation, Tom was feeling good, talking to wife, and suddenly dropped over dead. The blood clot hit his heart.

I continued to run the hardware store for his wife, Hazel. We carried a profitable stock, including some plumbing fixtures, pipe, faucets, and fittings. Our only unprofitable part of the business was the toy section. Kids would come in and go through those toys, tear them up, and toss them in the garbage. Most parents would deny their kids broke anything, and we took the loss. We hired someone just to take care of the housewares and toys. Still, it was a losing proposition. When I took over management, I got rid of those toys.

Louie Merley, a friend who was an excellent mechanic and had worked for me at Wide Ruins on the Kohler, agreed to connect a burglar alarm for us in the jewelry and pawn department of Hart Hardware. He installed an electric eye, and, if the beam was broken, a big bell rang on the outside and inside of the store. It worked perfectly to protect the front door. I rigged up some ropes and pulleys that would set off the alarm if anyone opened the back door.

We had a partner in the pawn shop, Mr. Tobe Turpen. He was a good friend who originally loaned us the money for the pawn shop. When Jean and I went to Hawaii on our twenty-fifth wedding anniversary, I asked Tobe to check on the store occasionally. The Navajo women, Juanita and Marie, who were clerks in the pawn and jewelry department knew how to shut off the alarm. There were no problems until Tobe came to check on things and walked right into the jewelry and pawn department. Well, all hell broke loose! The Indian clerks had to shut it off for him.

Tom's wife, Hazel, owned the store. I'd get enough money in to pay the bills, and she'd come up from Wickenburg, looking for cash, and clean it out. No way you could run a business with somebody cleaning out the money once in a while like that. We'd be behind a month paying our bills. We could get a 2 percent discount on orders if we paid by the tenth of the month. But with Hazel taking all that money, it ruined our chances for any discount and for having a growing business.

By that time, I was helping Jean in the pawn shop, which we owned, along with Jean's Jewelry. She was a very successful manager and the one who made the money for our family. I quit taking a salary in the hardware store for seven years in order to try and save the business for Tom and Hazel. I would borrow about twelve thousand dollars every year in personal loans and put it back in the hardware store to keep it going and try to get it out of debt. I used that money mainly to pay off the still existing mortgage on the hardware store, somewhere around thirty thousand dollars, as well as some old accounts that we'd been making payments on. So the hardware was still in debt to me, but the mortgage and other creditors were paid off. I finally got a note from the corporation, signed by Hazel, for the money due me for the loans.

After Tom died in 1968, I continued trying to make the business profitable. Then, one day, Hazel had been to Phoenix and found a diamond ring she wanted. She came up to Gallup and took eight hundred dollars right out of the store saying, "Why not? I deserve it." That was the last straw for me, and I decided I could no longer work for free. Running a business and not making any money is a despicable thing. That's when I told her I would buy or start my own business. I'd had enough. And Jean agreed.

I said, "Look, Hazel, I can't work for nothing any longer. I want to work for myself. I will buy your hardware store, building, and merchandise. And you will be out of it. I'll pay you cash."

She said, "Give me thirty days to think about it, then we'll talk it over." When the thirty days was up, I tried to reach her by phone and never could.

A few days later, a friend of mine said, "Hazel's in town. Didn't you know it?"

"No." I was damned angry. She was staying with friends and didn't even have the courtesy to contact me and discuss the possibilities, even to say yes or no.

I jumped in the car and drove over to where she was staying and confronted her: "I've got to have an answer. Am I going to buy the hardware store? What are we going to do? It's up to you."

She said, "Well, you talk to my lawyer."

"Okay. Who's your lawyer?"

"Mr. Perry."

"I'll be glad to." I went to Mr. Perry's office about 9:00 in the morning. I'd never had any man treat me as nasty as he did.

"You couldn't make any money for them in the hardware business," he said. "How are you going to make any money for yourself? But I guess that's none of my business."

"That's right," I answered. "It's none of your business, but I'm going to tell you why." And I explained about all her withdrawals and the way she kept the plumbing out of the business. "I don't need the hardware store. I'm going to quit and Hazel can sell it to someone else. I'd *prefer* that she sell it to someone else beside me. But I'm not going to continue working for her. I've been working seven years without a salary. After she and Tom moved to Wickenburg, she'd come back and take four or five thousand dollars out of the checking account a couple of times a year. You can't run a business that way, but it's her store and there's nothing I can do about her taking that money. I even took a personal loan for the store every year."

The lawyer said, "I'm going to have those books audited."

And I said, "Fine. If there's anything I can do, I'd be happy to help. And if you can sell it to someone else, I'd prefer it. But I made an offer and I'll stick with it."

So Mr. Perry called an auditor, who just laughed. "I've looked at these books for Hart Hardware every year," he said. "There's nothing wrong with them. Working under the conditions Bill Cousins has, it's no wonder he's struggling."

The lawyer audited the books again and, of course, found nothing wrong. After that, Mr. Perry became as friendly as a lost puppy. About then, my corporation note came due, and I got myself an attorney, Mr. Lebeck, who called Mr. Perry and said, "I hope we're not going to have any problems over the money owed to Bill on this corporation note."

"Oh, no," Mr. Perry said. "There will be no problem. He will get his money."

Hazel was angry because she was losing the one person who would work for free and also take a personal loan to keep the hardware store afloat. That was hard for her to give up, so she refused to sell me the building. She sold it to Walter Schanuel for two thousand dollars less than I offered her. She tried to sell the merchandise but couldn't. The other offers were too low compared to my offer. I had done an inventory and offered her 30 percent more than the others had offered. Finally, she decided to sell it to me. So, between the merchandise and other property that she and Tom had sold, plus Tom's insurance, Hazel wasn't left penniless.

In 1971, Jean and I rented another building for our store and started Cousins Hardware and Indian Jewelry. Jean's pawn shop was located in the back and turned out to be very

Cousins Brothers, circa 1950s. Left to right: Tom, lived to be sixty-eight; Bill, still going strong at eighty-six; Malin, lived to be seventy-seven; and Bob, lived to be eighty-six.

successful. When Jean wasn't busy, she'd work in the hardware business with me selling merchandise, and I would help her in the jewelry department. We built our business up until we were selling to dealers all over the country and one in Germany.

We kept an old-time hardware store and concentrated on getting vintage merchandise, like a horse harness. Not many people sold harnesses in the 1970s. We sold horse collars and buggy whips. We even had a real buggy. Jean tells how we got the buggy from an Amish farmer back east. That buggy was a curiosity to many people, who would come in just to see it after we restored it to look brand new.

We'd scour the country for any kind of antiques we could find, like Daisy hand-cranked churns. We even had a cream separator. These items were mostly for display, but everything had prices and eventually we sold it all. We were the only ones

Cousins Hardware and Jewelry, 1971.

in town who had crockery. They were good drawing cards to get folks into the hardware store and, once inside, they generally bought something.

We sold every size of nail and stored them in bins. There were twenty-four different types and sizes. We even had a calf blab, a contraption that fit in the calf's nose to help wean it.

We sold curry brushes and combs for horses. Once, a certain clerk who worked in the store came over to me and said, "I sold a curry comb and brush. We've only got one of each left, so I put them on the Want Book." The Want Book kept our list of supplies to order next.

"Sure, that's good," I said. "While you're over there, did you check on the curry powder?"

"Oh, gosh," he said seriously. "I never thought about that."

He looked for it and finally returned to tell me, "I never seen any curry powder at all, so I'll put it on the Want Book, too." I never told him I was pulling his leg and that curry was a spice you could only get at the grocery store.

A government man came into the store one day and went directly over in the paint department and picked up a can of Deer-O Paint, made by a company in Phoenix. They were one of our oldest distributors, and we liked their paint. "Can I help you?" I asked. He looked at me, looked back at the paint, but didn't say a word. I didn't like his attitude, so I simply said, "Well, if there's anything I can help you with, just give me a growl." I walked away.

"Wait a minute." He reached into his pocket and flashed a badge. That automatically made me mad because I could see that he wanted to show his power. He said he was with the EPA, checking on ingredients of the paint we were selling. "I'm especially interested in gym floor seal," he said.

I knew that he was looking for the lead content in paint. "We don't have it."

"My information says you do," he insisted.

"I don't give a damn what your information says, we don't have any." I was getting madder by the minute.

"Would you show me your invoices?"

"Yes, sure." I said and told my bookkeeper, Mary Husband, to show him the invoices from Deer-O Paint Company.

She gave them to him, and he went through them for twenty or thirty minutes. Finally, he said, "I guess you're right. I don't see an invoice for gym floor seal."

"I told you we didn't handle it."

"Well, I'm going to pick up some paint, anyway, and sample it for the U.S. government."

"All right," I answered. You can buy anything you want. Everything here is for sale, so pick whatever you like."

"We generally give the dealer his cost plus 10 percent. That's all we do."

I was real mad by now. "Mister, if you take any paint, or anything else out of here, you'll pay full retail price, plus sales tax."

"The government doesn't pay sales tax."

"Then you'd better be prepared to hand me a tax-exempt form if you expect not to be charged any sales tax." By that time, I was so mad I was just shaking, so I walked away. My son, Edward, stepped in to take over.

The agent asked, "Does he really mean that?"

Edward nodded. "I'm sure he means every word."

So the agent relented and Edward sold him fifty to sixty dollars of paint at full retail price. After that, we never had any trouble from government agents.

I remember one incident when I walked up the street to Woodard's Indian Jewelry to see Tommy Woodard about something. While I was there, a lady came in who was with the National Park Service running the jewelry department in a gift shop at Mount Rainier National Park. I couldn't help but overhear the conversation. Woodard told her that the only way they could do business was for her to buy at least two thousand dollars' worth of merchandise, and her check had to be back by the tenth of the following month. They couldn't carry it any longer. She explained that she couldn't work that way because the government required a purchase order and the whole process took at least sixty days to turn around. Woodard wasn't interested.

I couldn't say anything right there in Woodard's store, but I sure hoped she would come down to our place. I went back and told Jean what I'd heard: "By golly, I wish we could get that account. I know we could work with her."

A little later, the front door of our store opened, and that same woman walked in. She explained her purchasing situation to us and asked if we were interested in working with her. We said we'd be happy to do business. She bought between three and four thousand dollars' worth of merchandise from us that day. Just as she promised, we were paid within sixty days. Over the years, that turned out to be one of our better accounts. We enjoyed a profitable business with the park service for many years.

One fall, we had an extra good piñon crop and decided to send some to our dealers. We filled bags with about eight to ten pounds of piñons and mailed them to all of our dealers. We got letters back thanking us for the coffee, or some called them beans, and wanting to know how to cook them. No one seemed to know what the piñons were. Then we had to write to everyone and explain what the piñons were and how to crack and eat them. We thought everybody knew what piñon nuts were, but we found out differently.

We had some friends up in Minnesota who ran a curio shop, selling Indian jewelry and other items of the area. They sent us several pounds of wild rice that the northern Indians picked from their canoes. We loved it, even though we had enough wild rice to last for all the holidays and every day in between.

We considered all of our customers to be "nice people," even when they weren't so nice, because they were customers and that's the way we treated them. Once an Indian man came in and said, "My wife wants a hammer." He named the brand.

"Sorry," I said, "We don't have that brand. We sell the four best brands and have lots of good hammers, but not that one."

He insisted that he wanted that particular brand, saying, "This is for my wife. She says this is the kind she wants. And you know how the womans are."

I just answered, "Boy, do I ever!" And I wasn't able to help him.

We sold lots of stainless steel mixing bowls, water pails, and cooking pots, the bigger the better. One day, some Indian women came in and looked at the twelve-quart pails and said, "Don't you have anything bigger?"

An employee commented, "If we had pots as big as bathtubs, they'd want them bigger." Well, that was the wrong thing to say, because it offended them. They almost walked out of the store.

My son, Edward, was working in the store that day and stepped up. "I'll take over," he said. Somehow he soothed their ruffled feathers and sold more than three hundred dollars' worth of goods to them.

We also carried lots of large, two-feet-high cast iron kettles, the kind that sit on legs. Over the years, it became practically impossible to buy them, but luckily we found a supply with a foundry in Kentucky called Belknap. Not only would Indians buy them, but dealers would buy them from us. One asked, "What do the Indians use them for?"

I answered, "That's what they put preachers in. When they get enough of these preachers who come out on the Reservation, they cook them and eat them." From then on, those kettles were known as "preacher pots." I bought them from Belknap until the company wrote me that they were no longer making these pots and I wouldn't be able to get any more. I must have been about their only customer for those large pots.

Belknap was a wholesale house in Louisville, Kentucky, that sold hardware to many dealers in Gallup. They had merchandise that you couldn't get anywhere else, like the preacher pots. I wrote them a letter and asked if they would send a salesman to my store because I wanted to buy some merchandise from them. So they sent a salesman out, and we placed an order. At least a month passed, and still no hardware was delivered. I wanted to know what had happened, so I told

Jean, "Let's go to Albuquerque, catch a plane, and fly to Kentucky and see why our merchandise hasn't come." I always felt it was better to do business with a person face to face, and this gave us a good excuse for a little trip.

So we flew out there and got a room in a hotel in Louisville. The next morning, we could see the Belknap Hardware store out the window, so after breakfast, we walked over there. It was seven stories high with forty-seven acres of floor space. We told the elevator man that we wanted to see the manager of the order department. He took us up to the top floor. We walked in and introduced ourselves. The manager was very nice and said they'd shipped our merchandise the day before, COD.

"Why did you do that?" I asked. "We don't buy things COD. We send a check just as soon as we get the invoice."

He said, "We couldn't find that you had a credit rating in Dun and Bradstreet, so we couldn't do business on credit."

"We don't have a rating," I answered, angry that they would check on me. "I don't think we need one. But I sent you a list of references. Have you contacted any of them?"

"No. I didn't see it."

"Look on the back of the order."

He turned it over and there was Deer-O Paint Company in Phoenix; Blishmize and Sillman in Topeka; Mumpson, Dunnigan and Ryan, also Zork Hardware in Albuquerque; and Arizona Hardware in Phoenix. These were all companies that we'd done business with for many years. When we got a bill from them, we paid it right away and got our 2 percent discount, which amounted to a lot of money with as much as we were ordering.

The manager apologized and said, "We'll open an account for you, so that from now on, you can buy on credit. Will you go ahead and pay the COD this one time?"

"Yes," I agreed. "But don't ever send anything COD again." And they never did. We had a nice relationship with them for many years after that, until we closed the hardware store.

Our hardware store was not the neatest place. We'd have a barrel of chains, a keg of nails, a set of dishes, all side by side down the aisle. We handled all sizes of chains and boomers to tighten the chains on trucks.

I put up a bunch of signs to get a few laughs. Instead of "Wet paint" signs, I had "Dry paint" signs. The store had only one restroom for both sexes, and we kept it locked all the time because drunks would come in and throw bottles down the commode and stop it up, as well as become a general nuisance. So we kept the key and only let our customers use it. One of the signs in the bathroom said: "Smile. You're on Candid Camera." That got a lot of laughs and a lot of worried ladies.

Mirrors sold very well also. My sign next to them said: "Please do not look in these mirrors. They're brand new, and we don't like to sell secondhand merchandise. If you look, be prepared to buy."

A sign in my office read: "Let's not be an *out-house*. Put it on the Want Book." We didn't want to have to tell customers that we were "out" of some item.

Another sign read: "We take cash, sell on credit, take checks, and take gold, but we don't take goldbricks. We've got enough of those as it is."

We also sold oak whiskey barrels that I got from a company in Albuquerque. These fifty-gallon barrels had about a half-pint of whiskey left in them, and they smelled strong. One of our salesmen, Mr. Ruckman, sold calendars, gift boxes, Christmas cards and the like. We usually placed a large order for these products. Before he left the store, I generally gave him a good shot of whiskey. Later, he would go out to Bob's trading post at Cousins Brothers and tell him, "I give Bill a hard time, but he always gives me a nice shot of whiskey."

One day, after we'd conducted business, I gave Mr. Rucker the usual shot of whiskey. Just as he was leaving the store, I called him back. "Wait just a minute. Before you leave, would you like to smell a bung hole?"

"What?"

I figured he didn't know what it was. "How about a smell of this bung hole?"

"What do you mean?"

With a screwdriver and hammer, I knocked the bung out of the whiskey barrel and told him to take a sniff. He got quite a charge out of that and agreed to have another shot of whiskey—but not out of the barrel—before he went on to Bob's.

In 1980, after working for ourselves for nine years, Jean and I decided to retire. We had worked long and hard all our lives and figured it was time to relax a little. And move on to something new.

A Life Well-Lived

By this time, Jean was ill with emphysema, but her optimism and continued quest for learning and finding beauty in life remained strong. Bill's love for her was poignantly expressed in the ultimate acts of caring for her during this period. When Sallie Lippincott wrote the Foreword for this book, we first learned that Jean had been writing the family history since the Wide Ruins days. Even her immediate family didn't know it. Everyone assumed that she began recording the family history after their retirement. Even in the 1940s, she felt that theirs were stories worth telling and a history worth preserving.

Both Jean and Bill Cousins express happiness with their life together, in hard times and good, and reveal through their life experiences their indomitable pioneer qualities and contributions to the spirit and history of the Southwest.

Introspection

It is gratifying for me to see so much progress since I came West in 1925, when my mother taught Navajo adults to speak English. Now the young Navajo men and women are taking responsible positions in most fields of our society. One thrilling event for me was to see a thirteen-year-old Navajo girl advance to the finals in the national spelling bee in 1992. In my opinion, she was truly a winner, regardless of her standing. To quote Dr. Ruth Underhill, anthropologist, "They [the Navajos] are in a transition period, but aren't all of us?" The transition continues, as in all cultures.

On a recent trip to Gallup, we stopped by our daughter Ruth's shop. She now owns the Indian jewelry and pawn shop that I started, continuing the trading business that her grandfather Cousins began one hundred years ago. Many of our old friends and customers came in on business while we were there. We visited, and they brought me up to date on their families. I was so happy to see them all.

What great experiences our years of trading gave us, as well as so many memories. We lived in a most wonderful era, from horse and wagon to trains, automobiles, planes and trips to the moon. I hope our children can have as much progress and fun as we did, and that our happy memories can live on.

Sums It Up

In July 1980, Jean and I decided to retire. We wanted to have a little fun for the rest of our days. We closed out the hardware merchandise and liquidated the stock. Our daughter, Ruth, bought the pawn and jewelry business, then moved it to 2000 E. Highway 66, where she continues to run Cousins Indian Jewelry and Jean's All-Indian Pawn Shop, Inc. Ruth had worked in the store with Jean for about four years learning the business end of it, and after she took over, Jean and I assisted her for several months until she got established. Then we surprised everyone by selling our home on Maple Street in Gallup and moving to a beautiful little retirement community in Concho Valley, Arizona.

When we told Ruth that we were going to sell our house and move to Concho Valley, she was like me when Wide Ruins was sold. She'd just turned forty, and her life was changing completely. She couldn't believe it. She thought we were crazy to leave the security of family and friends in Gallup for a rural area far from doctors, a hospital, or other conveniences. But we were used to that kind of lifestyle from all those years of working on posts. We liked the peace and quiet of country life.

The next weekend, Jean and I went with Bob and Betty Cousins to Concho Valley, to find a place to live. We looked at several houses until we found just the right one. It was located on a hill with a beautiful view overlooking Concho

Valley on one side and a huge ranch with nothing but a few cattle on the other. The house had more than two thousand square feet, with a large living/dining room, three big bedrooms, two baths, a nice kitchen, and walk-in closets—just beautiful, with everything we needed and more. It was truly a long way from those humble little places we lived in when we first got married.

We bought the house, joined the country club, and planned to relax for the rest of our lives. We met new neighbors, who soon turned into good friends. We enjoyed playing cards and golfing every week and had a great time fishing in the beautiful lake fed by one of the largest natural springs in Arizona. Our life there was wonderful for a few years. Then Jean began to feel sick all the time.

We took her to several specialists, who all said she had the first stages of emphysema. Their advice was, "Quit smoking." The doctor in Gallup put her on oxygen sixteen hours a day with instructions to stop smoking.

Even though we had both smoked cigarettes for almost fifty years, I said, "Well, we'll just quit smoking right now. Neither of us will smoke anymore." Jean looked at me pretty hard. I didn't realize until later that she was such a heavy smoker. We went down to rent an oxygen concentrator and headed home to Concho. On the trip, about five miles southwest of Zuni, Jean reached into her purse and lit a cigarette. I watched her but didn't say a word. She took two puffs and threw the cigarette out the window.

I had smoked cigarettes since I was ten or twelve years old, but, of course, my folks didn't know it at the time. So it was hard for me to give up smoking, too, but I quit along with Jean. After about three or four days of no smoking, and I walked into the bedroom and Jean was sitting on the bed, crying.

"What's the matter, honey?"

"I want a cigarette."

"Let's go another day. Just one more day without."

The next day she said, "Well, it's another day, and I still want a cigarette."

I knew she was desperate for a cigarette because I was, too. So I came up with a plan. "All right, I'll tell you what. Every night about five o'clock, let's sit out on our front porch in comfortable chairs and have a scotch and water with a cigarette before dinner."

"What does that have to do with stopping wanting a cigarette?"

"We'll each have a cigarette. We'll have that one time to look forward to all day."

"Oh, great." She wasn't too happy with the plan but agreed. That evening, we each had a scotch and water and our one cigarette for the day. We smoked the damn thing to the nub. For about a month, that one cigarette was all we had each day. Finally, we reached the point where we didn't even care about it. We just threw our cigarettes away and quit smoking altogether. But we didn't give up the scotch!

Finally, Jean got so sick that we had to move back to Gallup, where she could be close to medical care. She only lived a couple of years there and died February 7, 1993. It was the saddest day of my life, the day I lost my Jean.

Jean's dream was to see the stories of all our lives made into a book. I never thought it was possible until recently, but she believed that we lived in a special time. Now I see that she was right. I've worked hard on this to see her dreams come true. We had a long and happy life together.

NOTES

Roots

p. 7: *Intertribal Ceremonial:* Jean noted, "The idea for the present-day Ceremonial held in Gallup started with Mike Kirk, brother to John Kirk. Both Mike and John Kirk were old-time traders, and we later worked for John at Borrego Pass. Mike, who lived in Manuelito, New Mexico, about twenty miles west of Gallup, was quite a showman. At one time, he and a group of performing Indians traveled around doing shows called 'First Americans,' similar to Wild Bill Hickock's."

p. 8: *arts and crafts:* "The fine arts they bring today are of far better quality and skill than in those days," Jean stated.

p. 8: *New Mexico Civil Service:* This service later became the Bureau of Indian Affairs.

p. 13: *Chee Dodge:* Chee Dodge became the first elected chairman of the Navajo nation.

p. 15: *S. E. Aldrich:* Stephen E. Aldrich was an early trader, dating to 1884 tent trading. He was a former cavalryman and veteran of the Apache campaigns. He built Round Rock Trading Post and Sehili Post.

p. 15: *Charles Weidemeyre:* Charles Weidemeyre was an early trader who founded the Gallup Mercantile Company, a wholesale house for traders. The present-day spelling of Chinle occurred in April 1941.

Chin Lee, Whitewater

p. 25: *Monuments:* They are now known as Spider Rock.

Notes

p. 27: *valley store:* This site is now Many Farms.

p. 33: *The Checkerboard Area:* comprised of land of varied ownership, for example, state, federal, reservation, and privately owned.

p. 44: *in the Cousins family:* Presently, Malin's only daughter, Grace, and her husband, Grant Wheatley, run the trading post.

Thunderbird Post, Chin Lee

p. 53: *delayed honeymoon:* Jean remarked, "A few years later, for our twenty-fifth anniversary, we borrowed two thousand dollars and took off for Hawaii. We had a wonderful time and felt we deserved it, and long overdue."

p. 57: *He denied it:* Bill commented, "Years later, the phone company surveyed for phone lines along section lines. They found that the farmer had moved the corner stone and made him move his fence back. That road, Cousins Road, exists today, with the jog still there."

p. 59: *John Fussbuttons:* Bill added, "Later, he was a customer of our daughter Ruth's in the Gallup store for a number of years."

p. 60: *they had a whole bunch of kids:* Bill recalled, "Many years later in Gallup, Joe Mance brought Jean some beautiful belts to pawn. He even kept them with our daughter Ruth in her store in Gallup. After he died, his daughter, a granddaughter, and one of his wives came into the store to claim three beautiful old belts of his that were very well made. None of them had a pawn ticket, which was not surprising since he always lost the ticket. Legally, the pawn shop dealer must see that ticket in order to hand over merchandise in pawn. Ruth knew who it belonged to but didn't want to get in the middle of this family argument. So she said, 'No one can have these belts until you get together, stop arguing, and put in writing to me who should get which belt. Otherwise, those belts will become dead pawn.' That meant someone else could buy them. Well, the family didn't want that, so they did as she asked and she distributed the belts to the named members of the family."

p. 67: *George Bloomfield:* George Bloomfield was an early trader who greatly influenced the improvement of the quality of Navajo rugs during that era and the development of the Two Gray Hills-style rug.

Borrego Pass Post

p. 92: *he dismantled the whole thing:* Bill noted, "Betty Cousins still has that very piano in her home at Cousins Brothers Trading Post."

God's Little Acre

p. 98: *great neighbors:* Jean continued, "Many years later, in the late seventies, Bertha and I still enjoyed our friendship. She went to Albuquerque to make her home with a daughter, and George was killed by a retarded son some time back."

Wide Ruins

p. 125: *Beatien Yazz:* He also signs his work B. Yazz or Beatian Yazz.

Wide Ruins: Tales and Times

p. 151: *prehistoric village site:* Ronald P. Maldonado, *An Archaeological Inventory Survey of a Proposed Roads Construction Project, Prepared for Bureau of Indian Affairs, Ft. Defiance Agency, Branch of Roads* (Washington: Government Printing Office, 1993); J. W. Powell, *Report of the Bureau of American Ethnology 1900-01* (Washington: Government Printing Office, 1904), p. 124.

p. 153: *letters:* The letters in this section are reproduced character for character from the originals. The reader should bear in mind that English was not only a second language to these Navajos, but also, quite probably, the only written language they had ever used.

p. 163: *Ansel Adams:* The only verification that Ansel Adams was the photographer is Jean Cousin's memory, which we have no reason to doubt. An inquiry to the University of Arizona's

Notes

Center for Creative Photography, the largest archieve of Adams's work, produced no record of a negative. Possibly (and quite probably), Adams discarded it because it was never published as far as we know.

p. 179: *red:* This is Bill's term for "Communist."

p. 180: *problems of the time:* Several factors impeded making a living in a trading post on the reservation at that time. The availability of cars and trucks made the society much more mobile, and the Navajos could go to town and didn't have to rely so completely on the post. Also, the Navajo tribal council wanted to impose strict guidelines for running the business, including special taxes for the traders that could not be passed on to the customer.

Gallup Business

p. 189: *Asa Glascock:* Glascock was as well-respected businessman in Gallup who ran a city trading post.

p. 190: *R. M. Bruchman:* Bruchman was a wholesaler in Winslow, Arizona.

p. 192: *Shalako dance:* This was an all-night blessing ceremony performed by the Zuni Pueblo Indians.

p. 197: *Jean's All-Indian Jewelry and Pawn Shop:* The shop has been known by several names: Jean's Jewelry, Jean's All-Indian Jewelry and Pawn Shop, and, later, Cousins Hardware and Indian Jewelry. The present-day shop, located at 2000 E. 66 Ave., Gallup, is Cousins Indian Jewelry and Jean's All-Indian Pawn Shop, Inc.

p. 211: *Kohler:* Bill refers to the Kohler Light Plant, an electric generator used at Wide Ruins for the Post and homes located there.

p. 214: *Walter Schanuel:* Schanuel was a Gallup businessman who ran the Western Auto Store. The building was finally razed, and a parking lot occupies the space.

Bibliography

Barnes, Will C. *Arizona Place Names.* Tucson: University of Arizona Press, 1988.

Hegemann, Elizabeth Compton. *Navaho Trading Days.* Albuquerque: University of New Mexico Press, 1963.

"Historic Trading Posts." *Plateau Magazine* 57 (1986): 10-17.

James, H. L. *Posts and Rugs: The Story of Navajo Rugs and Their Homes.* Globe, AZ: Southwest Parks and Monuments Association, 1976.

Morgan, Anne Hodges, and Strickland, Rennard, eds. *Arizona Memories.* Tucson: University of Arizona Press, 1984.

McNitt, Frank. *The Indian Traders.* Norman: University of Oklahoma Press, 1962.

Noe, Sally. *Greetings from Gallup: Six Decades of Route 66.* Gallup, NM: Gallup Downtown Development Group, 1980.

Richardson, Gladwell. *Navajo Trader.* Tucson: University of Arizona Press, 1986.

Roberts, Willow. *Stokes Carson, Twentieth-Century Trading on the Navajo Reservation.* Albuquerque: University of New Mexico Press, 1987.

Rodee, Marian E. *One Hundred Years of Navajo Rugs.* Albuquerque: University of New Mexico Press, 1995.

Roessel, Ruth, and Johnson, Broderick H., eds. *Navajo Livestock Reduction: A National Disgrace.* Chinle, AZ: Navajo Community College Press, 1974.

Young, Robert W., and Morgan, William. *Navajo Language Grammar and Colloquial Dictionary.* Albuquerque: University of New Mexico Press, 1980.

Index

DATE DUE

GAYLORD			PRINTED IN U.S.A.